"This book is a must-read for anyone wan
became so unhealthily attached to a toxic pe
sonal power and integrity."

> —**George Simon, PhD,** author of the international best-seller,
> *In Sheep's Clothing,* and *Character Disturbance*

"Shahida Arabi masterfully educates readers about the complex intersection of neuroscience and the intricacies of healing in the aftermath of psychological abuse. Written in a style that is digestible, informative, and packed with research, Shahida's book will no doubt serve as an essential guide for survivors and helping professionals alike. Bravo, Shahida!"

> —**Andrea Schneider, MSW, LCSW,** licensed clinical social
> worker/psychotherapist in the San Francisco Bay Area, and
> author of *Soul Vampires*

"Shahida Arabi's work has contributed mightily to our understanding of how to help victims identify, avoid, and escape from toxic narcissists and psychopaths. Her latest book, *Breaking Trauma Bonds with Narcissists and Psychopaths,* brilliantly outs the dynamics of such exploitive, destructive people. Her guidance on escaping from ensnaring narcissists is the most comprehensive I have ever read. Anyone who reads it will be aided greatly in avoiding or breaking trauma bonds."

> —**Pete Walker, LMFT,** traumatologist, and best-selling author
> of *Complex PTSD* and *Holistically Treating Complex PTSD*

"A transformational book for survivors of narcissistic abuse, it provides a killer combination of impeccable research, science, and case studies to reassure readers that what happened to them was no one-off or in any way their fault, and, additionally, that the distress they feel is not an 'overreaction,' but the measurable effect of trauma on their brains—which can, happily, be gradually reverted by doing the healing work Arabi outlines."

> —**Annie Kaszina, PhD,** coach, founder of www.
> recoverfromemotionalabuse.com, and author of *Married to
> Mr. Nasty* and *The Woman You Want to Be*

"*Breaking Trauma Bonds with Narcissists and Psychopaths* is a vital resource for survivors seeking to reclaim their mental and emotional well-being. Shahida's insightful guidance empowers individuals to break free from the destructive cycles of manipulative relationships. With clarity and compassion, this book provides a road map for detaching from toxic bonds and rediscovering inner strength. A must-read for those ready to break free from the grips of trauma and reclaim their sense of self."

> **—Lisa A. Romano,** life coach and award-winning author specializing in codependency and narcissistic abuse recovery

"Readers will find validation and clarity in Shahida Arabi's science-based, research-backed analysis. They will also encounter a knowledgeable and compassionate guide who provides hope and the important steps to begin to support the self-awareness necessary to break through the disorientation and fragmentation that accompanies this kind of destructive relational dynamic, and ultimately return to wholeness."

> **—Gretchen Seitz, DAOM, LAc,** owner of Seitz Acupuncture and Integrative Health

Breaking Trauma Bonds

with Narcissists and Psychopaths

Stop the Cycle of Manipulation, Exploitation, and Abuse in Your Romantic Relationships

SHAHIDA ARABI, MA

New Harbinger Publications, Inc.

Publisher's Note

NEW HARBINGER PUBLICATIONS is a registered trademark of New Harbinger Publications, Inc.

New Harbinger Publications is an employee-owned company.

Copyright © 2025 by Shahida Arabi
New Harbinger Publications, Inc.
5720 Shattuck Avenue
Oakland, CA 94609
www.newharbinger.com

All Rights Reserved

Cover design by Amy Daniel

Acquired by Jess O'Brien

Edited by Karen Levy

Library of Congress Cataloging-in-Publication Data on file

Printed in the United States of America

27   26   25

10   9   8   7   6   5   4   3   2   1   First Printing

Dedicated to my beautiful and brilliant mother, Rehana, a talented math professor and storyteller who shaped my love for learning early on and helped me become the researcher and writer I am today, as well as to my wonderful readers who have supported me throughout the years.

Contents

Introduction

You've likely come across this book because you're searching for answers. Your tumultuous romantic relationship, friendship, familial relationship, coworker, or boss makes you feel uneasy. You think you might be experiencing manipulation, but you struggle with self-doubt. You question whether the confusing person in your life meant to hurt you or whether you're overthinking things. You have a gnawing sense that something is not quite right and you may even feel like you're going crazy—or even being *driven* crazy by the toxic person in your life. Yet you feel unable to detach from the situation, always drawn back to and ensnared by the same destructive cycle with the person who hurts you the most. You seek comfort from the person that has harmed you, even if you know it doesn't make sense.

Does some of this describe your situation? If so, you're not alone. Millions of people all over the world have felt what you may be feeling right now. They, too, have experienced what is known as a *trauma bond*—an unhealthy, intense attachment we can form to toxic people as a survival mechanism that can, paradoxically enough, negatively affect our safety and well-being.

Toxic relationships take a toll on the mind and the body. If you've experienced chronic manipulation, you've likely found yourself walking on eggshells and questioning your emotions and experiences—even your perception of reality. You may feel exhausted, tense, and helpless—it's difficult to concentrate and focus on your goals because you're caught up in the chaos this person orchestrates in your life. You have experienced numerous transgressions, betrayals, and violations—and you have been trained to abandon and betray yourself by staying in the relationship.

You feel like you love this person, yet the relationship betrays everything you know about the nature of healthy love. It's a perversion of what a healthy relationship should look like, but you have developed a habit of rationalizing and minimizing the red flags and overriding your own boundaries and standards. You find yourself constantly comparing yourself to others and forgetting your own irreplaceability and uniqueness. You've lost your sense of self.

Breaking the Trauma Bond and Healing Are Possible

It can be difficult to free and heal yourself of these destructive ties, but it's more than possible. In this book, you'll learn how to identify the red flags of manipulators, such as individuals with narcissistic and psychopathic traits. In the first few chapters, you'll read extensively about the research behind why destructive personalities do what they do and the traits and behaviors that can cause you to become entrenched in a cycle of abuse. You will learn in-depth information about how the trauma of such a relationship affects the brain, what a trauma bond entails, and the psychological and biochemical addiction we can develop to toxic people, which is what makes it so difficult to break ties.

The second half of this book explores the evidence-based healing modalities and therapeutic tools that can help you on your journey. You will also learn how to empower and heal yourself with powerful exercises that help break the trauma bonds that keep you tied to dangerous partners, friends, family members, and business associates. Many of the exercises provided are available for download at the website for this book here: http://www.newharbinger.com/53561. You may also want to keep a journal to record your thoughts and feelings as you read through this book.

Although this book is focused on romantic relationships, the same tips can be adapted and applied across the board to different contexts and a diverse array of relationships, such as in your extended family, friendships, and the workplace. I hope in this book you find healing, validation, and freedom—validation in knowing you are never alone, healing in the steps I show you to take back your power, and freedom from the toxic people and trauma bonds in your life.

CHAPTER 1

Trauma Bonds with Dangerous People

Mabel met Tony at a work conference. He was charming, handsome, and swept her off her feet. Every week he would send her flowers with sweet "love" notes. The relationship moved quickly with exciting dates, romantic getaways, and long conversations that lasted for hours. Mabel felt like she had met the love of her life: Tony and her shared so much in common.

Within five months, Tony had moved into Mabel's apartment. Once he got comfortable, however, Tony "changed." He refused to contribute to the rent, even though that had been the agreement. His personality was no longer loving, caring, or affectionate—he was cold and contemptuous. He would no longer greet her warmly at the door as she was accustomed to. He stopped answering her calls when she called him on her lunch break. He was no longer the productive worker bee he presented himself to be and stopped going to the office. He would sit around at the apartment doing drugs that he never disclosed to Mabel he used, and even began bringing his ex-girlfriends and affair partners over to the apartment she was paying for.

Mabel later found out he was never employed to begin with and had actually used a friend's badge to attend the conference where they first met. When Mabel confronted him about these issues, Tony responded in a violent outburst. She was shocked. She had never seen this side of him before. He promised he wouldn't do it again. She found herself pleading with him to get better and suggested he attend rehab. She took it upon herself to help him get back on his feet.

Tony seemed "better" for a while. But then, like clockwork, he would begin making insulting comments and evading questions about his job search. Mabel soon realized that Tony expected her to take on all of the financial and domestic responsibilities while making her an emotional punching bag in the relationship. Yet she tried harder to regain his approval and affection, suggesting couples therapy. She wanted to go back to the way the relationship used to feel in the beginning. Tony agreed to go but painted her as "clingy and needy" to the therapist, avoiding all accountability for his behavior. Even when the relationship ended, Mabel continued to agonize over what had happened and where it "all went wrong."

What Is a Trauma Bond?

All over the world, millions of people feel inextricably bonded to romantic partners, family members, friends, bosses, colleagues, and community leaders who repeatedly harm them. Perhaps you feel this way as well. This is known as *trauma bonding* or *betrayal bonding*. These terms describe the dangerous phenomenon where a victim of abuse, mistreatment, or exploitation feels inexplicably attached to their abuser out of a need to survive and maintain the traumatic relationship.

Although the example above illustrates a case where the victim is a woman, anyone of any gender or background can become trauma bonded. Victims who are trauma bonded find themselves biochemically and psychologically attached to the abuser in ways that make it difficult to leave the relationship. Trauma bonding can cause the victim to tolerate escalating mistreatment because they are forced to stay focused on their own survival rather than setting healthy boundaries. Survivors who are trauma bonded rationalize increasingly toxic behaviors, maintaining the relationship because they feel unable to protect themselves otherwise. Some victims who are trauma bonded develop the need to defend and protect their abusers to their family members, friends, and even law enforcement.

It's important to remember that trauma bonding has little to do with the actual merits of the abuser, or how "strong" the victim is. Even the strongest of people can become trauma bonded to an abuser who has subjected them to chronically cruel and callous treatment. My hope is that as you read this book, you will better understand trauma bonding and identify the tactics manipulators use to keep you tied to them. But in order to break the trauma bond, you first have to recognize you are bonded in the first place.

How a Trauma Bond Forms

In order for a trauma bond to form, there usually has to be the presence of intermittent kindness, a power imbalance, and the presence of danger and betrayal (Adorjan et al. 2012; Wallace 2007; Dutton & Painter 1993). The person who holds more power in the relationship tends to mix periods of kindness with cruelty, subjecting their victim to horrific betrayals that shatter their sense of self. The victim becomes conditioned to trying to gain the approval of the perpetrator in order to survive the trauma of the relationship, forming an intense attachment known as the *trauma bond*. Behaviors that stem from the trauma bond might look like apologizing to the abuser when you've been the one harmed to try to "win" back their approval, refusing to press charges against someone who has committed a crime against you, continuing to work for a boss who first charms you and then exploits you, or remaining in contact with a family member who has mistreated you and continues to push boundaries.

In the realm of abusive relationships, narcissistic and psychopathic individuals can create very powerful trauma bonds and attachments due to their disorienting manipulation tactics and intermittent devaluation and praise. They display a lack of empathy, an excessive sense of entitlement, malicious envy, and often a lack of remorse. These behaviors and traits can drive a number of betrayals and violations throughout the relationship. For instance, in Mabel and Tony's relationship, Tony felt entitled to move into Mabel's apartment and not financially contribute while he cheated on her and used drugs in her home. He essentially exploited

Mabel for her resources and also disrespected her and violated her when she held him accountable.

The addictive nature of these dysfunctional relationships can take a toll on both mind and body. As we'll discuss throughout the book, neuroscience research indicates that toxic "love" and adverse-ridden relationships create a euphoric and addictive bond that affects victims of abuse biochemically, tethering them to those who mistreat them. Dopamine, the "feel-good" neurotransmitter in the brain, flows more readily when the "rewards" in the relationship are intermittent and unpredictable, causing us to work harder for the "fix" we experienced in the initial honeymoon stages of the relationship (e.g., Fisher et al. 2016; Schulze et al. 2013). Over time, this might look like the abusive partner withholding affection for no apparent reason or disappearing randomly at times and then returning without explanation, causing you to doubt yourself and work harder to capture their attention.

Does some of this sound familiar? These behavior patterns and accompanying chemicals in the brain are partly why victims in abusive relationships with narcissists and psychopaths find it so difficult to extricate themselves from these destructive ties and struggle to detach from their toxic partners both during the relationship and in the traumatic aftermath.

Narcissistic People Can Create Powerful Trauma Bonds

Trauma, and the effects of trauma, also play a powerful role in maintaining these tumultuous connections. As a researcher, I've had the privilege and honor of investigating and developing a better understanding of this phenomenon through working with survivor populations. In my 2023 large-scale research study of people in romantic relationships with narcissistic and psychopathic individuals, published in the journal *Personality and Individual Differences*, I established the first empirical association between narcissistic partner traits and post-traumatic stress disorder (PTSD) symptoms specifically related to the relationship (Arabi 2023).

There are two subtypes of narcissism: grandiose and vulnerable. Grandiose narcissistic traits relate to superiority, high self-esteem, entitlement, and dominance, while vulnerable narcissistic traits are characterized more by hypersensitivity and low self-esteem. Both were predictors of PTSD, with grandiose narcissism being the strongest predictor in the study.

It's no surprise that individuals in romantic relationships with people who have narcissistic and, to an extent, psychopathic traits would experience PTSD symptoms. These traits are associated with aggression according to a wealth of research, such as a meta-analysis of 437 independent studies (Kjærvik & Bushman 2021). In other words, if you are in a relationship with someone with narcissistic traits, there's a high likelihood that you may develop PTSD—and that PTSD symptoms may be keeping you bonded to your partner.

You may be thinking, *How do I know it's the narcissistic partner that caused PTSD and not my childhood trauma or other past relationships?* Often, society judges abuse victims and tries to minimize the severity of the trauma that can result from being in a relationship with a narcissist. To ensure my study did take other possible factors into consideration, I accounted for the partner's history of childhood abuse, other previous abuse, their partner's manipulation tactics, and physical abuse in the relationship. I found that it was the *narcissistic traits* of their partner that had a greater effect than these variables and most strongly predicted the PTSD symptoms of participants, even when the impact of these other variables was assessed.

I also discovered that these partner traits predicted two specific PTSD symptom categories the most: intrusion and avoidance symptoms. As survivors struggle with intrusion symptoms, such as intrusive thoughts, flashbacks, and nightmares related to the relationship, and maladaptive avoidance strategies to ward off both internal and external reminders of the trauma, they may feel even more "bonded" to their perpetrators. Not only are they attempting to battle the effects of the traumatic relationship and struggling in ways that make self-care difficult, but they are also subconsciously coping in ways that avoid facing the true nature of their partner, the relationship, and its most painful aspects. As you'll learn later in this chapter, this form of denial and avoidance can be a key component of traumatic bonding and a deterrent to healing.

Bonding and Betrayal

Along with PTSD symptoms, these types of relationships are rife with traumatic or betrayal bonding. This means you feel a need to survive the numerous betrayals, violations, and transgressions within the abusive relationship. These betrayals and their accompanying manipulation tactics can hook you into investing in a toxic person. As we'll discuss more in depth, manipulation tactics can include love bombing (the excessive flattery, praise, and attention used to ensnare you at the onset of the relationship) followed by abrupt debasement. Your partner may also purposely try to make you jealous to gain power and control. Both manipulation tactics were found to predict PTSD in my study, albeit on a smaller scale (Arabi 2023). A narcissistic person may demean you or subject you to manufactured love triangles to keep you in a constant state of confusion and competition. These manipulation tactics paradoxically create even stronger bonds as you work harder to regain their attention and affection after you've been ensnared in their abuse cycle.

While society often poses the question "Why didn't you just leave?" it's clear that abuse has an impact on the ways you process and deal with betrayal. The betrayals that often break ties in "normal" healthy relationships are the very ones that can bond you more closely with narcissistic and psychopathic individuals. Such betrayals represent a threat not only to the survival of the relationship but also to your own psychological survival because these relationships are set up early on to produce intense attachments and unhealthy enmeshment. Through the disorienting nature of their manipulation tactics and shifting states of adoration and callousness, a narcissistic or psychopathic partner can convince you over time that your identity and very sense of self are dependent on them. They erode your self-esteem until you become hyperfixated on their perception of you, and you become conditioned to engage in compulsive behaviors to try to fix that faulty perception and the relationship.

Relationships with such personality types often contribute to severe cognitive dissonance—an ongoing battle between your conflicting beliefs, thoughts, and emotions about who the abuser really is. They erode your identity until your very sense of self is overridden by the abuser's perception. You may experience emotional whiplash, where you walk on eggshells due to the unpredictable nature of the abuser and feel struck and blindsided by their harmful actions. There are multiple forms of destructive conditioning and maladaptive survival mechanisms involved to both maintain the relationship and your own sense of psychological and even physical survival in such a tumultuous, chaotic relationship. These manipulation tactics and the very nature of a relationship with a narcissist are essentially "rigged" to bond the victim to the perpetrator.

What Is Betrayal Trauma and Bonding?

What we now understand about trauma bonding has its origins in the concept of betrayal trauma. These two terms, betrayal bonding and trauma bonding, can be used interchangeably, as they describe the same dynamics, although "betrayal bonding" places more of an emphasis on the effects of the betrayals that survivors endure in producing attachment to the perpetrator. Researcher Dr. Jennifer Freyd first introduced the term *betrayal trauma* in 1991 and *betrayal trauma theory* in 1994 to illustrate how the experience of being betrayed by someone we are dependent on can change the way the brain cognitively processes and encodes the betrayal. This shapes the degree to which the betrayal is available to our conscious awareness (such as the spontaneous suppression of physical or psychological pain for the purposes of perceived survival) and drives our psychological and behavioral responses toward doing whatever it takes to cope, including maintaining the destructive relationship (Freyd 2008; Gómez & Freyd 2019). This is because "detecting betrayal" can be dangerous and lead to "costly outcomes," such as overwhelming pain, loss of resources, and disruptions in mental or physical health, so you repress your initial reactions to the betrayal and prioritize your survival (Gómez & Freyd 2019). For example, if you share children with your narcissistic partner, or were isolated by them to become financially dependent on them, you will be more likely to tiptoe around confronting them or asserting yourself, and more likely to try to please them in an attempt to keep your family intact or maintain access to vital resources. Similarly, if your relationship is a physically abusive one, the fear of physical retaliation can cause your brain to become focused on how to avoid angering the abuser rather than exiting the relationship in an attempt to avoid violence.

As Gómez and Freyd (2019) note, although normally cutting ties with someone who has betrayed you is an evolutionarily advantageous response, it can appear *disadvantageous* to your survival when the person who has betrayed you is also someone you are dependent on for survival and resources. For example, an abusive parent can withhold food or shelter from their child, a sex trafficker can take you hostage and threaten your life, or an abusive intimate partner can make you emotionally and financially dependent on them.

Stockholm Syndrome and Trauma Bonding

The term *Stockholm syndrome* points to a special kind of betrayal trauma where people begin to experience positive feelings for their captors, presumably as a coping mechanism to survive (Cantor & Price 2007). It was first coined by psychiatrist Nils Bejerot in 1973 to explain the bonding that occurred between victims and captors during a six-day hostage situation amidst a bank robbery in Stockholm, Sweden (King 2020). Not only did the four hostages develop positive feelings and seek approval from their two captors, but they also resented police for coming to their rescue and did not try to obtain freedom even when the opportunity arose. Stockholm syndrome can include experiencing PTSD symptoms, a perceived inability to escape, developing "appeasement" styles of catering to the perpetrator to avoid abuse and punishment, and developing a heightened gratitude for the small kindnesses the captor throws your way. This is what therapist Joe Carver (2014) calls "the small kindness perception," and it's also prevalent in abusive relationships.

Similarly, you may defend your perpetrator furiously and even resent friends, family members, or authority figures who attempt to intervene in the relationship. This can be partly due to your fear of retaliation from the abuser, who seeks to control and isolate you and will punish you for gaining any kind of perceived social support. Perhaps you've defended your partner numerous times to your friends and family members who've expressed concern about the fact that you seem overwhelmed and constantly on edge from this toxic relationship. Yet deep down, you have a feeling that their concerns are valid and that you may be in a dangerous situation that you feel unable to get out of. Being in a trauma bond can make you feel absolutely exhausted, helpless, and drained. Staying in the relationship can seem easier than leaving because you might fear both emotional consequences and physical retaliation that could ensue if you do leave. The abuser has programmed you to feel like you "need" them.

The widespread nature of betrayal or trauma bonding cannot be underestimated. Dr. Patrick Carnes (2019) notes that betrayal bonds can create obsessive, tormented relationships forged in treachery. Betrayal bonding can occur in a number of different contexts, such as cases of incest and child abuse, dysfunctional marriages, cults, spiritual and religious abuse, kidnapping, hostage situations, and exploitation in the workplace. This betrayal trauma is not just limited to the most extreme circumstances that signal immediate danger; it can also create what Freyd calls a kind of "betrayal blindness" (Johnson-Freyd & Freyd 2013) to infidelity, workplace inequity and discrimination, or other forms of institutional betrayal.

EXERCISE: The Trauma Bond Checklist

Now that you've learned more about trauma bonds, consider the checklist below and identify any of the following that best describes your situation. You can also download this checklist at http://www.newharbinger.com /53561.

☐ The relationship started out with intense amounts of attention, affection, and praise. Now, it has shifted into hot-and-cold behavior that devalues and minimizes you, demeaning the positive qualities your toxic partner once praised, triggering your worst insecurities, and manufacturing new insecurities that never existed prior to the relationship.

☐ You're rarely sure which "version" of this person you're going to get and find yourself walking on eggshells, trying to prevent their anger, and managing their moods to try to "predict" their actions.

☐ You feel addicted to the relationship, even when it feels dangerous. You may know this person is toxic for you, but a part of you feels inextricably attached to the person they presented themselves to be in the beginning of the relationship.

☐ Incidents of abuse, mistreatment, or betrayal in this relationship tend to be followed by periods of love bombing, displays of remorse, or hollow apologies, only for the cycle to begin again.

☐ You've developed an intense preoccupation with this person and find yourself constantly thinking about them, fantasizing about them in loving ways, or feeling intense anger toward them. You may vacillate between these two states and find it difficult to understand or pinpoint who this person really is or how you authentically feel toward them.

☐ You find yourself minimizing and rationalizing incidents of cruelty, emotional or physical abuse, and betrayals, especially ones you found unacceptable before.

☐ You engage in compulsive behaviors to connect to, communicate with, or check up on this person, even when it seems irrational or harmful to do so.

☐ You have overwhelming evidence that your partner is harmful, deceptive, or conniving, but you can't seem to let go of the relationship.

☐ You may have tried several times to leave the relationship, but your partner has convinced you to come back or you have found it difficult to detach entirely. You may have left the relationship multiple times, only to go back to the abuser when they promised to change.

☐ You find yourself doing everything to please them and are loyal to a fault, even when they don't reciprocate.

☐ You defend your abuser to people who express concern about your partner and the relationship. You may still do "favors" for your abuser or go out of your way to try to regain their approval.

☐ You find yourself constantly overexplaining yourself to your abuser and other people, attempting to rationalize your valid emotions and reactions because of the intense amount of manipulation you've endured.

☐ You have begun engaging in self-destructive or reckless habits as a result of this relationship or even self-harm.

☐ You have lost your sense of self, worth, and value.

☐ You compare yourself to others due to the abuser's constant attempts to provoke jealousy. You have become dependent on the abuser's perception of you, even going so far as to try to "correct" this perception.

Your Brain on Trauma and PTSD

You may wonder why you feel so out of control in a trauma-bonded relationship. We will talk more about what neuroscience tells us about narcissistic and psychopathic pathology in the next few chapters. But first, it's important to understand how *your* brain works differently in a toxic relationship with a pathological personality, or in any abusive relationship in general, especially when you are suffering from symptoms of PTSD. While there may be individual differences, generally trauma can affect the brain in specific ways that create chaos in learning, memory, and decision making. Let's explore how trauma can create changes in the following areas of the brain.

Amygdala

The amygdala is a small, almond-shaped structure located in the limbic system, which processes fear and emotions. It activates our fight-or-flight response in times of threat and danger, playing a key role in keeping us safe. Neuroscience research tells us that for trauma survivors, the amygdala tends to be highly active yet smaller in volume. In studies, the amygdala becomes highly activated when someone with PTSD recalls traumatic memories or recounts their traumatic experiences, or begins to associate fear with a certain trigger. This could mean that the amygdala is working overtime trying to process extremely emotional, traumatic experiences (Bremner et al. 2006). A smaller amygdala is also associated with greater fear, heightened anxiety, and a more intense stress response (we talk more about this stress response in the section on the HPA axis below).

PTSD also affects how the amygdala connects to and communicates with other parts of the brain. Research shows the link between the amygdala and the prefrontal cortex, known as the more "rational" part of our brain, is disrupted in people with PTSD. Because the prefrontal cortex (discussed in more detail below) is vital to our decision making, judgment, focus, and planning, it helps regulate the amygdala in a "top-down" processing manner. This keeps the amygdala under control and balanced when it comes to our emotions and fear so we don't get too overwhelmed. Along with signals from other parts of the brain—such as the hippocampus and the striatum, which help with learning, memory, habit formation, motivation, and reward—the prefrontal cortex figures out when there are threats in our environment and guides our responses to that threat. With PTSD, however, the prefrontal cortex's activity is diminished; the amygdala's activity is heightened, and it can even overcommunicate with the striatum, making habitual reactions to trauma cues even stronger (Elliot & Packard 2008). The amygdala thus takes a front seat during trauma, firing off signals to produce stress hormones that impair the function of the prefrontal cortex while intensifying the amygdala's response to stress when the trauma is chronic.

Basically, when we're traumatized, it's our "emotional" amygdala, the more reactive and primitive survival part of the brain, that tends to run the show, and our more rational "thinking" part of the brain goes offline. That's why you may feel unable to remain calm or make mindful decisions when dealing with a toxic partner. Understanding all this can help you put your compulsive unhealthy habits and overwhelming fear responses into a greater context. When it comes to trauma and abuse, after all, your brain tends to work against you.

Prefrontal Cortex

The prefrontal cortex is essential for executive functioning. As mentioned previously, it plays a "top-down" role in regulating our emotions and contributes to our reasoning, decision making, insight about our actions and the actions of others, goal-directed behavior, impulse control, reality testing, judgment, and learning. If you notice that trauma affects your ability to focus, make decisions, and control your impulses, it's because it dampens the prefrontal cortex—it actually gets smaller and less active. Many survivors of abusive relationships note that during and after traumas, they had difficulty making decisions and focusing on their daily goals, and they became more prone to impulsive or reckless behavior. As you learned, this is because trauma decreases the prefrontal cortex's ability to regulate the amygdala, causing the brain to return to a more primitive, reactive state.

There is also a decreased response specifically in the ventromedial prefrontal cortex—indicating lower activation in an area associated with higher level executive functioning and decision-making processes—and a dysfunctional response in the anterior cingulate cortex, related to impulse control, cost-benefit calculation, motivation, emotion, fear responses, and decision-making (Etkin & Wager 2007; Shin et al. 2006). This can interfere with our learning, decision-making, and emotional regulation, and as a result, you may be less able to regulate your emotions and control your impulses, or make rational decisions that accurately assess the costs and benefits in toxic romantic relationships.

Hippocampus

Have you noticed a loss or disruption in your ability to remember abusive events? This is no coincidence—it's because trauma also affects the parts of our brain that deal with learning and memory. The hippocampus is located in the temporal lobe of the brain and is vital to learning and memory, especially long-term memories that can be recollected verbally, as well as fear conditioning (the process by which fear becomes associated with a certain trigger) and the stress response. The hippocampus helps to store and retrieve memories, yet chronic stress can impair it. You may wonder why you struggle to express the abuse you are experiencing or recollect the full extent of the abuse you endured, yet find yourself overwhelmed by vivid recollections or flashbacks of specific traumatic events. This is because trauma can affect the processes of encoding memories, recalling and retrieving memories, and how memories are stored and consolidated in the brain, creating fragmentation. The emotional intensity of the traumatic event can interfere with how memories are stored and remembered, which can also be affected by the aberrant processing of memories in areas of the brain like the amygdala, which can contribute to fragmented sensory details, sensations, and images of the trauma, and the hippocampus, which stores and consolidates memories of events and helps create coherent narratives of the memory (Costa 2022). The amygdala also shows dysfunctional interactions with the hippocampus and with other brain regions related to the processing of body sensations, visual processing, and the processing of emotional information after trauma and during memory recall (Belleau et al. 2020).

A recent study showed that traumatic memories differ from regular memories since people who are re-exposed to the details of their traumatic memories actually experience activation in the posterior cingulate cortex, not the hippocampus, indicating these experiences have not been properly consolidated and organized in the hippocampus—and this was associated with greater PTSD severity (Perl et al. 2023). The posterior cingulate cortex deals with processing an internal experience, and researcher suggests that survivors experience the traumatic memory as if it were happening in the present moment. That is why you may feel especially on edge when you suddenly "flashback" to the sights, scents, or sounds of a traumatic event—it's like a memory that hasn't been fully processed yet as a coherent narrative, so it comes back on a loop, especially when faced with triggers of the original trauma causing survivors to feel as if it were happening in the present moment than the past. The disruption in communication between the emotional and rational parts of your brain during and after trauma only strengthens this sense of fragmentation. If there is dissociation (a trauma response where you feel separated from your body or the world) and intense emotions during the traumatic event (known as *peritraumatic dissociation*), memories can also become fragmented and less coherent, and survivors are more likely to experience PTSD symptoms and a subjective sense of fragmentation (Bedard-Gilligan & Zoellner 2012; Ozer et al. 2003).

Stress can also slow down neurogenesis, the birth of new neurons, in the hippocampus and inhibit an important protein called brain-derived neurotrophic factor (BDNF), which helps with the growth and survival of new neurons (Begni et al. 2017). This can interfere with your ability to learn new things and cause mood changes or even depression. Trauma and prolonged stress may also shrink the hippocampus and reduce communication among neural cells through the loss of dendritic spines, the tree branch–like projections extending from neurons that help pass on information between neurons. Thankfully, there are healing modalities that can help us rewire the brain toward the direction of healing, which we'll discuss in chapter 4.

HPA Axis

Do you experience sleep disturbances, fatigue, brain fog, weight gain or loss, loss of appetite, and even a weakened immune system? Perhaps you don't have the energy to even get out of bed, let alone find healthy ways to detach and leave a toxic relationship? These can be the result of trauma's impact on your brain and its impaired stress response. Our brain is uniquely adapted to confront temporary danger and threats in our environment, but it isn't always adaptive when it comes to confronting an abusive relationship, where the threat is always present. What happens when the danger is always there?

The hypothalamic-pituitary-adrenal (HPA) axis refers to our stress response system, which manages communication among the hypothalamus, pituitary, and adrenal glands. The HPA axis releases important hormones that provide energy for the fight-or-flight response—to help us fight or flee when we're in danger. Think of a woman suddenly seeing a bear in the wild. Her pupils dilate, her breath quickens, she sweats, her heart rate increases, and her muscles tense. These are physiological responses to a perceived threat.

When we see or hear an incoming threat, our amygdala acts like the conductor of an orchestra, sending a signal to the hypothalamus, the part of our brain involved in producing hormones that control our body temperature and heart rate to "begin the show," activating our fight-or-flight response. Our sympathetic nervous system sends signals to the adrenals to release the "troops" and prepare for battle. The adrenals release the hormone epinephrine (adrenaline), which flows into our bloodstream and causes our heart to beat faster, thus delivering more blood to the muscles, heart, and vital organs, and allows for our lungs to take in more oxygen. Our pupils also dilate to let in more light—our vision sharpens—and our digestion slows down so we can conserve all our energy. These signals occur so instantaneously that they happen even before our brain has fully visually processed the threat, so we can instantaneously react in order to survive.

Such a fight-or-flight response can occur not just because of a physical threat but also from emotional dangers and triggers, especially in PTSD, where your triggers can cause you to relive the same traumatic experience over and over again. This is why you may feel always on edge around your abuser, especially during and after the early stages of betrayal. Your brain is constantly trying to fight off potential "attacks" or violations and anticipate the next threat around the corner.

If the threat is still present even after adrenaline subsides, the hypothalamus needs to continue to work with the sympathetic nervous system to keep us alert and alive. The show isn't over yet. So, the hypothalamus then releases additional soldiers for battle, including cortisol. This handy hormone mobilizes the body to respond to stress. Cortisol is an important part of the HPA axis that helps support our survival. After the stressful event is over, the stress response is "complete," cortisol levels fall, the parasympathetic system hits the brakes, and we return to baseline.

At least, we are supposed to. But if stressors are occurring on an ongoing basis, it acts like a Trojan horse that covertly creates a more invasive sense of threat: the HPA axis and its responses can continue to be activated, and our stress response can become disrupted even after the threat is over. In the case of an occasional stressful event in an otherwise peaceful life, this stress response can be very helpful. But if you are living in that same stress every day, mired in the same danger or threat over and over, then your body may feel like you are being pursued by a bear on a daily basis (in this case, the "bear" in your life is actually your narcissistic or psychopathic partner psychologically or even physically attacking you). This causes excess anxiety and affects your ability to cope.

Unfortunately, an overactivated stress response leads to consequences for the brain. For example, excess stress hormones can damage neuronal structures in the amygdala, prefrontal cortex, and hippocampus, which, as you learned, are the areas of the brain vital for learning, memory, critical thinking, and emotional balance. You can also become so sensitive to hormones released during the stress response that they become amplified even in response to stressors that are seemingly minor. For example, we might find ourselves very triggered by a coworker raising their voice slightly at us because we have experienced the major stress of a manipulator lashing out in a rage attack in the past.

On the other hand, once we become habituated to the same type of stress over and over again, for some individuals, there's also a chance of having a *decreased* release of stress hormones, which might desensitize us to the stressful event. Desensitization in an abusive relationship can be dangerous as our body no longer "raises the alarm" every time an abusive incident occurs. In order to "mobilize" us to fight back or flee the threat, we would need a *new* threat, but waiting around for that to occur could place us in even more danger.

Vagus Nerve

The vagus nerve is one of the major cranial nerves in your body that affects several organ systems. It's a vital part of your parasympathetic nervous system that halts your fight-or-flight response, instigates the relaxation response, and helps control mood, immune responses, digestion, and heart rate. Unlike the sympathetic nervous system, which revs up your body to fight a stressor, the parasympathetic nervous system pushes the brakes and tells the body and the HPA axis to calm down after a threat has passed. Trauma can create a weaker vagal tone, which can affect cardiovascular, autoimmune, and mental health conditions. You'll want to work more effectively with your distressed vagus nerve when it comes to healing the trauma bond (more on this in chapter 4).

Biochemical Addiction

As mentioned earlier, an essential aspect of trauma bonding is in the physiological as well as psychological bond we develop with our abusers— a kind of "addiction" that is strengthened and solidified by hormones and neurochemicals in the brain like dopamine, serotonin, oxytocin, cortisol, and adrenaline. We'll talk more about how these affect the trauma bond in chapter 3. Identifying this biochemical addiction and finding healthier, evidence-based ways to heal and regulate these addictive aspects will help you break free of these bonds.

Takeaways

If you find yourself relating to most of the behaviors and emotions in this chapter, take a deep breath. The first step to healing and detaching from the trauma bond is to understand how it works. This chapter explained how a trauma bond forms, how people with narcissistic and psychopathic traits manipulate this bond through numerous betrayals, and how the brain's structures and biochemical systems reinforce this bond.

Accepting that you are entangled in a trauma bond is one of the most difficult parts of the journey to come to terms with—knowing that the person you love and care so much about is causing you harm, yet you still feel attached to them. It's also a pivotal moment of transformation, holding the possibility for immense change. In the next chapter, you'll learn more about the manipulation tactics narcissistic and psychopathic individuals use to keep you attached to them.

CHAPTER 2

Identifying Narcissists and Psychopaths

When you are trauma bonded to a partner (or a friend, family member, colleague, or boss), you can feel hopeless and depleted. You may feel trapped and frightened, as if you have no options but to tolerate the relationship. You've probably been told by outsiders that what you have been through is just the "everyday" highs and lows of a romantic relationship, or led to believe that your abuser may change. Yet you feel incredibly traumatized and you know that the manipulation you endured is anything *but* normal. *Narcissist* and *psychopath* have become popular buzzwords, a kind of shorthand to describe manipulative and exploitative people who lack empathy. But these terms hold deeper meaning in clinical and research settings, and they are essential to have a greater understanding of if you want to understand what you just experienced. This validation and deeper understanding of these terms can help you pave the path to freedom and safety.

The Traits of a Narcissist

Narcissism, or "narcissistic," can refer to the traits and behaviors associated with the full-fledged disorder of narcissistic personality disorder. And if you've experienced a narcissistic individual—whether it's someone with "just" the traits or the full-fledged disorder—you will often know it. Studies show that contrary to popular opinion, the assessments of loved ones and family members of narcissistic people tend to be incredibly accurate and aligned with the ratings from experts on those same narcissistic people (Miller et al. 2005; Carlson et al. 2013). If you suspect you've been in a relationship with someone who has either narcissistic or psychopathic traits, don't minimize or doubt yourself.

The *Diagnostic and Statistical Manual of Mental Disorders, Fifth Edition* (American Psychiatric Association 2013) defines a narcissistic person as someone who has five (or more) of the following symptoms beginning in early adulthood and present in a variety of contexts:

- Has a grandiose sense of self-importance (e.g., they exaggerate achievements and talents, demand to be treated and recognized as superior without achievements that back up this false sense of superiority)

- Is excessively fixated on fantasies of success, power, brilliance, beauty, or ideal love

- Believes that he or she is "special" and unique and should only associate with other special or high-status people (or institutions)

- Requires heavy admiration and praise from others

- Has an inflated sense of entitlement (i.e., unreasonable expectations of especially favorable treatment or automatic compliance with his or her expectations)

- Is interpersonally exploitative (i.e., callously takes advantage of others to achieve their own ends)

- Lacks empathy and is unwilling to recognize or identify with the feelings and needs of others

- Is pathologically envious of others or projects this envy onto other people, believing or accusing others of being envious of them

- Shows arrogant, haughty behaviors or attitudes

However, "narcissism" as a set of traits rather than a disorder exists on a spectrum. Someone can potentially have many narcissistic traits and exploit others harmfully without necessarily meeting the full criteria for this disorder. And narcissism doesn't look the same across every person, so if you're struggling in a toxic relationship with someone who doesn't "seem" narcissistic by stereotypical standards, that doesn't mean your experience is any less valid. Someone can be narcissistic and boisterous and arrogant—or they can be quieter, more introverted, and more calculating. As mentioned earlier, researchers have also identified that there can be two types of narcissism: grandiose and vulnerable. Both grandiose and vulnerable traits can coexist within an individual, although some individuals may fit into one subtype more than the other. Yet according to research, both "normal" and "pathological" forms of narcissism are associated with aggression and bullying behaviors toward others (Kjærvik & Bushman 2021). We must therefore take the full spectrum of narcissistic traits seriously, from the garden variety and subclinical to the more malignant.

The Origins of Narcissistic Traits

Often, trauma-bonded survivors want to know: What caused this? Why were they so cruel? How could they have treated me this way? Was it because of their childhood? While the prevailing myth for a long time has been that narcissism is often caused by childhood trauma, there's been mixed and scarce support for that theory. In fact, research shows that narcissistic traits can be driven by *parental overvaluation* (overly spoiling and excessively praising a child, teaching them a sense of entitlement) rather than childhood maltreatment or a lack of parental warmth. That is not to say that in some cases there isn't parental maltreatment involved, but it appears that parental overvaluation plays a bigger role than suspected in predicting narcissistic traits.

A 2015 longitudinal study of 565 individuals by Brummelman and colleagues studied both adolescents and their parents. It showed that parental overvaluation, *not* lack of parental warmth, predicted narcissism over time. In another 2020 study of 328 individuals by van Schie and colleagues, being overvalued, overprotected, and experiencing lenient parenting styles were associated with higher traits of pathological narcissism, and being "excessively pampered" was associated with both grandiose and vulnerable narcissistic traits, unrealistic self-perception, and entitlement. Other research also shows that narcissistic traits don't significantly differ between groups exposed to traumatic events and groups that are not (Dragioti et al. 2012). The bottom line is that more research needs to be conducted, and the origins of narcissism are much more complicated than we would assume.

The Traits of a Psychopath

What happens when you're dealing with someone on the more dangerous and potentially violent end of the spectrum? Antisocial personality disorder is characterized by numerous deficits in empathy, conscience, moral decision-making, and impulsivity. An individual with antisocial personality disorder has a pervasive pattern of disregard for and violation of the rights of others; this can include traits such as failure to conform to social norms, deceitfulness, impulsivity, irritability, aggressiveness, and lack of remorse, with these behaviors occurring since age fifteen (American Psychological Association 2013).

In the *DSM-5*, antisocial personality disorder is noted as an umbrella term that can also be referred to as *sociopathy* or *psychopathy*. Sociopathy and psychopathy do not have their own separate diagnoses in the *DSM-5*. However, the term *psychopath* is used by researchers and clinicians frequently across correctional and legal contexts. The broader research literature distinguishes between antisocial personality disorder and the term *psychopath*.

Psychologists have argued that someone can hypothetically meet the criteria for antisocial personality disorder but may not be a full-fledged psychopath. For example, they may meet the criteria for violating the law but not necessarily have a lack of remorse. The *DSM-5* diagnosis of antisocial personality disorder emphasizes more law-breaking behavior, which may not apply to every psychopath. Psychopathy is better measured using Dr. Robert Hare's twenty-item Psychopathy Checklist-Revised (PCL-R), a measure that includes more of the callous-unemotional features of psychopathy. In short, not all those who meet the criteria for antisocial personality disorder will be full-fledged psychopaths.

In Hare and Neumann's (2005) four-factor model, psychopathy is further broken down into four primary dimensions:

Factor 1: Interpersonal: Superficial and glib charm, grandiose sense of self-worth, pathological lying

Factor 2: Affective: Lack of remorse or guilt, shallow affect, callousness, lack of empathy, failure to take responsibility for actions

Factor 3: Lifestyle: Need for constant stimulation, proneness to boredom, impulsivity, irresponsibility, promiscuous sexual behavior, parasitic lifestyle, lack of realistic goals

Factor 4: Antisocial: Impaired behavioral controls, early behavior problems, juvenile delinquency, revocation of conditional release, criminal versatility

Two of these factors, the interpersonal and affective, are especially important to consider when it comes to the interpersonal exploitation and aggression of the psychopath in intimate relationships, and it's the severity of the callous-unemotional traits in these two factors that also distinguish the psychopath from those with "just" the behaviors of antisocial personality disorder. For example, people with higher levels of Factor 1 traits of psychopathy tend to show diminished physiological and neural responses to cues that are meant to induce emotions, including cues that reveal the distress of other people (Patrick, Bradley, & Lang 1993; Benning, Patrick, & Iacono 2005; Seara-Cardoso & Viding 2015; Seara-Cardoso et al. 2016; Blair 2013). This lack of reactivity to the emotions and distress of others may be in part why psychopaths are able to engage in so much aggression against others without inhibition and without empathizing with their victims. However, keep in mind that this does not excuse their behavior. Ultimately, they know the intellectual difference between right and wrong, have the capacity to choose differently, and are still responsible for their choices.

The Neuroscience Behind Psychopathic Motives and Sadism

You may have noticed that the psychopath in your life was not only unable to empathize or be remorseful, but that they also committed egregious moral transgressions without thinking twice, engaging in lying, cheating, or other exploitative behaviors that would cause regular people to feel guilty and ashamed. Psychopaths reason differently when it comes to moral dilemmas. What fMRI studies suggest is that areas of the brain constituting the "moral neural network" play a key role in moral reasoning and are activated differently in psychopaths when they're considering moral dilemmas, in ways that may contribute to why they dehumanize and exploit others so easily (e.g., Kiehl et al. 2001; Rilling et al. 2007; Müller et al. 2008; Harenski et al. 2010).

For example, Decety and colleagues (2013) examined the neural responses of psychopaths to the distress and pain of others. What they discovered was shocking. When 121 incarcerated males viewed images depicting bodily injuries and were asked to take the perspective of another person suffering these injuries, they showed an atypical response in certain areas of the brain involved in empathy for pain, even though they showed a typical empathic response for themselves when imagining the injury happening to *them*. This study indicated that when psychopathic individuals imagine others enduring pain, there is *increased* activation in areas of the brain related to anticipation of reward and *decreased* activation in areas related to empathy. Psychologists have suggested that this may mean that psychopaths not only lack empathy for the pain of others but also take sadistic pleasure in witnessing or even causing the pain and distress of others. This is why you may have witnessed a psychopathic individual seem especially pleased to cause you pain or go out of their way to partake in actions they knew would harm you.

Psychopaths are also more likely to lie more frequently than narcissists, experience more positive emotions or "duping delight" and a thrill when they con others, and lie for no reason, whereas narcissistic individuals lie primarily for self-gain (Azizli et al. 2016; Baughman et al. 2014; Jonason et al. 2014). Individuals with higher levels of psychopathy also tend to have reduced activity in the anterior cingulate cortex when engaging in an opportunity for personal gain by using dishonesty (Abe, Greene, & Kiehl 2018). The anterior cingulate cortex is an area of the brain that is associated with response conflict—simultaneous neural signals that support competing responses—and would be otherwise helpful in more executive control when it comes to decisions. This suggests they may experience less distress and less reaction time when making decisions to be dishonest in order to be opportunistic. If you noticed patterns of chronic infidelity or pathological lying in a psychopathic individual you were involved with, you are not alone—this is quite common and tends to be associated with their duplicity and ability to lead double lives.

Primary and Secondary Psychopathy

There tends to be two main types of psychopaths: "primary psychopaths" seem to have been cold and callous since they were young and don't get stressed out easily; they also have traits of antagonism and fearlessness. Some of the individuals from this group may be found in more successful careers. Maybe they're the CEO of a company, a doctor, psychiatrist, or nurse who preys on vulnerable populations, weaponizing their position and authority to get ahead. Yet they come from a stable upbringing, so there doesn't seem to be a "reason" for why they are the way they are. These psychopaths are thought to be "born" rather than made due to their biological predisposition toward psychopathy.

Studies show that people with primary psychopathy tend to have higher levels of psychological well-being and emotion regulation, can follow social norms more readily, are less impulsive, and are less susceptible to stress (Eisenbarth et al. 2019; Sethi et al. 2018, Saltoğlu & Uysal Irak 2022). Primary psychopaths also tend to have fewer post-traumatic stress disorder symptoms and incidents of childhood trauma than secondary psychopaths (Kimonis et al. 2012; Tatar et al. 2012). This is why you may meet someone with psychopathic traits who does not have the traditional "childhood trauma" background and may even come from a loving family.

Then there is the hotheaded "secondary psychopath," or colloquially termed *sociopath*, the one who always seems to lash out with no impulse control, is often a career criminal or has a list of misdemeanors to their name, and may have been raised in a chaotic environment. Secondary psychopathy is characterized by higher levels of anxiety, impulsivity, and reactive aggression, and is influenced and shaped mostly by their environment. Both types can be violent and maliciously aggressive toward others, but one is just more likely to get away with it.

You may have noticed that the psychopath in your life doesn't fear consequences or react to punishment. There are some neurological underpinnings to the primary psychopath's fearlessness. Researchers Sethi and colleagues (2018) discovered different brain activation patterns and amygdala activation between individuals who had "primary" psychopathy and "secondary" psychopathy. Interestingly, the primary group demonstrated reduced brain activity in response to fear. The secondary group had reduced activity in brain areas that play a key role in fear responses, perspective taking, and deducing the mental states and emotions of others.

Both groups had diminished activity in response to fear in the brain area associated with the acquisition and extinction of fear conditioning as well as the regulation of emotions, which may explain why they don't fear punishment. However, the secondary group had *reduced* brain activity compared to the primary subtype during anger processing, suggesting they may be more fearful and likely more impulsive than the primary subtype. In the same study, the secondary subtype also had higher levels of childhood maltreatment, internalizing symptoms, suicidality, and aggression than the primary subtype.

It's important to understand the research behind the origins of these pathological types because you may be tempted to rationalize a psychopath's behavior and assume that they all emerged from a life of pain, and this can keep you entrenched in the trauma bond and a toxic relationship cycle. Once you understand a psychopath's limitations may not have to do with trauma at all, you are less likely to excuse it or hope to "fix" someone with these traits.

EXERCISE: Spot the Narcissist and Psychopath

Read the sample case vignettes below and see if you can spot who falls into which "category." This is a general exercise to help you better recall the traits associated with each personality type so you can better assess your own situation and set boundaries; it is not intended to be a diagnostic tool. You can also download this exercise at http://www.newharbinger.com /53561. The answers are at the end, but don't peek!

As a reminder, the categories we discussed include:

- **Grandiose narcissist:** Narcissistic individuals who have more grandiose narcissistic traits can be boastful, exude a false sense of superiority, and have higher levels of self-esteem. They genuinely believe they are better than others and like to create situations where they exert power and control over others.

- **Vulnerable narcissist:** Narcissistic individuals who have more vulnerable narcissistic traits tend to present as more introverted and neurotic. They may not appear to be as confident or have high self-esteem, yet tend to rage and lash out at perceived slights.

- **Primary psychopath:** People who possess more of the traits of the primary subtype of psychopathy tend to be more fearless, are less likely to have a history of childhood trauma, tend to be more successful, and are believed to have a stronger biological predisposition toward psychopathy.

- **Secondary psychopath:** People who possess more of the traits of the secondary subtype of psychopathy tend to be more fearful, impulsive, hotheaded, and anxious; they are more affected by their environment and engage in more reactive aggression. They tend to be the less successful type of psychopath as they break laws more blatantly and frequently. This is the type most similar to the traditional *DSM-5* definition of antisocial personality disorder.

1

Brad works as a therapist in a well-known wellness center in his city. Unlike his empathic peers, however, he did not enter the field for genuine reasons. He enjoys the sense of validation he gets from his clients praising him, as well as from manipulating others and planting seeds of self-doubt. He also likes the authority that is given to him in the role of being a therapist and the feeling of being adored by a client when he first love bombs them into feeling special. When he feels he is not praised enough by a client, he lashes out underhandedly and comments on one of the insecurities they disclosed during sessions to covertly demean them.

Whereas most therapists would feel anguished at hurting a client, Brad enjoys seeing them feel deflated and powerless. However, he picks his targets carefully, choosing those who are most vulnerable to his influence so they don't report him. This is also the pattern he follows in his romantic relationships as well— he often preys on young vulnerable men and women at bars and exploits them for sex while pretending to seek a relationship. He feels a euphoric high when he disappears after and they text him frantically. In his free time, he tries to sabotage those in his field and outside of it who are successful and stalks those who inspire his envy. Even though Brad lacks the empathy, knowledge, character, and skill set to be a genuinely helpful therapist, he feels entitled to be seen as "the best" and "the only" person who can help others and relies on his credentials alone to maintain power.

Which category do you think Brad falls in?

2

Tom is a "career criminal" who has been in and out of jail multiple times. Last time, he robbed his neighbor. This time, he plans to rob a store. He persuades his girlfriend, Linda, to go with him. When Linda refuses, he flies into a rage, assaults her, and sends her to the hospital. When the police arrive to arrest him, he tells them he just "lost control" and it won't happen again. However, this type of impulsive violence has happened many times in the past and Tom is likely to continue this pattern no matter how many times he goes to jail.

Which category do you think Tom falls in?

3

Miranda is a nurse who is well respected at her local hospital. She is charming, helpful, and always ready to "save the day." People automatically take a liking to Miranda because of her charm. What they don't know is that Miranda lacks remorse and spent her childhood and adolescence torturing animals and bullying other kids. Unlike her fellow empathic nurses, she became a nurse because it gives her a sense of power and authority. Her superiors always trust her when she spreads lies about her hardworking colleagues to prevent them from being praised or promoted. Suspiciously, she always seems to be around when one of her patients suddenly feels ill or becomes sicker. What people don't know is that Miranda is the one causing them to be sick in the first place. She often gives her clients the wrong dose of their medication or a different one entirely to make them feel fatigued. Then, when a reaction inevitably occurs, she sadistically watches them writhe in pain before she rescues them. She uses these hurt-and-rescue methods gradually, escalating over time so no one notices a concrete pattern. During her lunch breaks, Miranda also steals pharmaceutical drugs to sell on the side for extra income. In her spare time outside of the hospital, she writes sadistic, bullying comments on the social media accounts of the other nurses she's jealous of as well as strangers.

Which category do you think Miranda falls in?

Answers

1. Brad is most likely a grandiose narcissist.

2. Tom fits the criteria of a secondary psychopath or "sociopath."

3. Miranda fits the description of a primary and "successful" psychopath.

Narcissists, Psychopaths, and Aggression

Research on aggression tells us that both narcissists and psychopaths can engage in unprovoked, calculated aggression to meet their agendas. Much of the writing about narcissism theorizes that these people lash out when there is a threat to their ego. However, Park and Colvin (2014) showed that narcissistic individuals degrade others more than non-narcissistic individuals, even when a threat to their ego is absent. This has implications for what is known as *narcissistic rage*, excessive rage that results from a perceived slight, and suggests that individuals in romantic relationships with narcissists may bear the brunt of unwarranted, unprovoked aggression as well as ego-threatened aggression (Tortoriello et al. 2017).

Psychopathy is associated with aggression used to obtain profit or pleasure as well as sadistic violence. People who fall in the "intermediate" zone between narcissism and psychopathy can also aggress against others for sadistic reasons, as researchers Lenzenweger and colleagues (2018) note that sadism is a key feature of malignant narcissism (narcissism with antisocial traits). Interestingly, other studies report that individuals high in narcissistic and psychopathic traits tend to experience positive emotions when they view sad faces; they also use their *cognitive empathy*— their ability to assess the emotions, intentions, and desires of others on an intellectual rather than affective level—to more effectively manipulate others while lacking the true empathy to care about the harm they cause (Ali, Amorim, & Chamorro-Premuzic 2009; Wai & Tiliopoulos 2012).

This indicates that narcissists and psychopaths not only know what they're doing, but they also like it.

Reactive and Proactive Aggression

A 2021 meta-analytic review of 437 independent studies consisting of 123,043 participants by researchers Kjærvik and Bushman revealed that narcissism had a significant relationship with both aggression and violence. This relationship was significant for conditions where there was some sort of perceived "provocation," such as a person giving them a negative evaluation that could threaten their ego, reputation, or grandiose self-image. Some narcissists frequently engage in *reactive aggression* by flying into a narcissistic rage as a reaction to a perceived slight or "narcissistic injury," such as a person who criticizes them or their behaviors (which may very well be a warranted criticism, depending on the circumstances).

However, this link between aggression and narcissism remained significant even in conditions where there was *no provocation at all* and held true for all forms of aggression. This means that even if a narcissist hasn't received any criticism from anyone, they can still engage in aggression proactively (premeditated). The researchers defined *proactive aggression* as incentivized acts of aggression to obtain "money, status, power, reputation, revenge, [and] prestige" (Kjærvik & Bushman 2021). Thus, narcissists can instigate aggressive behaviors against someone they wish to demean—such as belittling someone they envy, engaging in sabotaging behaviors to remove competition, finding an excuse to rage at someone or "retaliate" against someone for surpassing them, and using others as an emotional punching bag to feel more powerful and in control. That does not necessarily mean the victim deliberately "provoked" the narcissist, but that the narcissist perceived a provocation and might have a hypersensitivity that does not accurately reflect the world around them.

The link between aggression and narcissism is also true for both vulnerable (covert) narcissism and grandiose (overt) narcissism, which suggests that regardless of whether a narcissist appears more shy, introverted, and fearful or outwardly pompous, self-aggrandizing, and self-confident, both types of narcissists can violate others. It also applies to both males and females and for both "normal" and "pathological" narcissism.

Forms of aggression narcissists engage in include:

- physical aggression—hitting, kicking, slapping, or other violent acts
- verbal aggression—using words to abuse, taunt, mock, and demean
- direct aggression—aggression that is instigated in your presence
- indirect aggression—aggression that occurs even when you are absent, such as the spreading of rumors or gossip to slander you through smear campaigns
- displaced aggression—aggression that may be intended for someone else but is instead projected onto an innocent person, such as a bystander or a loved one who becomes the punching bag for the narcissist, whether in real life or online (including cyberbullying)

If you've been violated by a narcissist, whether through reactive aggression or proactive aggression, it's important not to blame yourself. If you are dealing with someone with narcissistic tendencies and it's affecting your well-being, it's important to detach and *implement*, rather than just verbalize, healthy boundaries (verbalizing these to the narcissist may simply cause them to use that information to trespass them sadistically) and make a safety plan to exit the relationship or context that's harming you.

Neuroscience and Aggression

Neuroscience can help us understand the behaviors and traits associated with narcissism *without* excusing anyone from accountability. That's because we cannot point to neuroscience studies and definitively say, "So that's why they behave this way," because there isn't a way to definitively link causation to biology or environmental influences. Behavior and the brain interact—experiences shape and change the brain and the brain is also able to shape behavior. We know, for example, that meditation can "rewire" the brain for more effective emotion regulation if it's a habit that is consistently utilized over time, and even increases gray matter density in areas of the brain related to learning and memory, while decreasing gray matter density in the amygdala, the hub of emotion and fear (Hölzel et al. 2010; 2011).

Because the brain is "plastic," narcissists can also learn certain behavioral patterns over time that activate and change their brains in specific ways. For example, a narcissist who is prone to getting their way and who receives a rejection or denial may show heightened brain activity in areas associated with emotion dysregulation or reward because they are accustomed to responding to situations that threaten their sense of entitlement with aggression to intimidate others—and may even feel rewarded by this. This is a behavioral pattern that has served them, so their brain may react in a specific pattern to meet their agendas. Or they may be biologically predisposed toward frustration intolerance—but they still choose to behave in a manner that harms others rather than using adaptive coping skills.

It's also not true that narcissists can't control their behavior. In fact, as you learned, studies report that they possess cognitive empathy, the ability to identify and understand the emotional states of others (Wai & Tiliopoulos 2012). However, they weaponize that cognitive empathy to better manipulate others. They lack the affective empathy to care or be willing to care. We know very well they can turn on the charm when they need to in order to persuade key stakeholders into doing what they want, and that they can rapidly change their behavior in front of witnesses. Thus, we must look at their behaviors not in the context of uncontrollability but rather as a set of behavioral patterns that stem from the need to control others. These patterns may be more "hardwired" and show up as differences in the brain.

Why Narcissists Lack Empathy, Emotion, and Fear of Punishment

Now that you know the brain can change and that it isn't necessarily the cause for someone's behavior, consider how neuroscience can still shed light on behavioral patterns of those who behave more aggressively or exploitatively toward others. Narcissistic personality disorder has been shown by fMRI studies to be connected to gray matter abnormalities in brain areas associated with emotional empathy, impulse control, decision making, and inhibiting inappropriate emotional responses (Schulze et al. 2013). Structural differences (like reduced thickness of the frontal cortex, responsible for our executive functioning) abound in areas of the brain related to emotion regulation, self-processing, and social cognition (Mao et al. 2016; Nenadic et al. 2015). Narcissists are also *less* likely to "catch the emotions" of others via the phenomenon known as emotional contagion (Czarna et al. 2015).

People with high narcissistic traits tend to score higher in what is known as *alexithymia*. This means they can struggle to identify and experience emotions. Brain-imaging studies reveal that during empathy-related tasks, there's less activity in areas of the brain associated with empathy (Fan et al. 2011). There also seems to be atypical functioning in the amygdala and prefrontal cortex when narcissists process emotions and fear (Feng et al. 2018). Clinical psychologists think this could help explain why narcissists display differences in reacting to and dealing with emotional situations and why they exhibit deficiencies in emotional processing and empathic functioning (Ronningstam & Baskin-Sommers 2013).

However, the brain is not the "final" say in our behavior. Our habitual choices and decisions also affect the way our brain can be activated, and we know from research that certain activities, like meditation, can affect thickness in cortical areas of the brain over time. Thus, our ingrained behaviors and the activities we engage in voluntarily on a daily basis also shape how our brain reacts. Rather than claiming, "It's because of their brain!" and taking away all accountability, we must acknowledge that while brains can differ across various psychopathological conditions, our environment and our voluntary reinforced behaviors and habits also have the power to shape the brain. Neuroscience provides us one lens to look at narcissism, but it isn't the whole picture.

When it comes to punishment, narcissists are similar to psychopaths. Those who scored higher on narcissistic traits specifically exhibit fewer indicators of emotion and attention in anticipation of or in direct response to aversive stimuli (any kind of unpleasant event, such as extreme heat or cold, loud noises, or pain), as well as lower anxiety (Kelsey et al. 2001). This means they may have less of a response to punishment. That could contribute to why punishment and consequences may feel less impactful for them, and they often continue in their behavior uninhibited by these concerns unless it directly affects the needs of their ego. Because they have such a high need for self-aggrandizement, they often feel slighted when their ego needs are not met.

Why Narcissists Feel So Slighted

A range of fMRI studies show that male narcissists specifically exhibit hypersensitivity in what is known as the "social pain network" of the brain, consisting of the anterior insula and dorsal and subgenual anterior cingulate cortex, areas related to motivation and emotion regulation (Cascio, Konrath, & Falk 2015). This network is associated with processing information related to oneself during incidents of social exclusion. Researchers theorize that this could be related to a narcissist's heightened sensitivity to criticism and perceived slights, causing interpersonal relationships with narcissists to be more draining, difficult, and conflict-ridden—especially for grandiose narcissists when they are faced with the discrepancy between their idealized beliefs about themselves and the reality (Jauk et al. 2017; Cascio, Konrath, & Falk 2015).

Female narcissists, too, may engage in retaliatory aggression in response to perceived social rejection. For example, a study conducted by Chester and DeWall (2016) explored *retaliatory aggression*, or aggression in response to perceived slights and interpersonal insults. They theorized that if narcissists behave aggressively due to a threat to their grandiose self-image and to reduce the discrepancy between the false image and reality, then areas in the brain that notice and detect such discrepancies would be activated during times of social rejection. This fMRI study revealed that when female narcissists displayed greater brain activation in the dorsal anterior cingulate cortex during social rejection, they indeed behaved more aggressively toward one of the rejecters by blasting them with an unpleasant noise when given the option to do so.

Again, this hypersensitivity seen in the brain and propensity toward retaliation are not excuses for their behavior. It's just a demonstration of how their brains may be activated differently. It may be that narcissists have practiced behaving in these patterns for so long that these activation patterns and neural pathways become even more "set." Thus, because they feel excessively deserving of the adoration and praise of others, when they do feel slighted, they lash out in inappropriate and demeaning ways to gain obedience from others. When they are rewarded and coddled for lashing out, this inevitably reinforces their behavior. And so the cycle continues.

Understanding the neuroscience behind narcissistic pathology can help you recognize that you are dealing with an individual who has likely had these behaviors hardwired in them since childhood, but it does not mean they should not be held accountable, especially if these behaviors reward them. It's very difficult to change someone like this or hope for change unless they are willing to seek help. Unfortunately, many narcissists and psychopaths do not fare well in therapy and actually become even more manipulative as they learn to effectively mimic empathy to exploit others.

The Need for Narcissistic Supply

You may wonder why the narcissist has such an insatiable need for attention. Primarily, narcissists seek narcissistic supply—sources of attention, ego strokes, resources—to bolster their grandiose sense of self and to gain power over others. Interestingly, narcissists exhibit disruptions in their functional and structural connections between areas of the brain involved in processing self-relevant information and those associated with reward (Chester et al. 2016). This may contribute to a disconnect that leads to finding "the self" unrewarding and may thus lead to overcompensation by trying to find excessive validation in the outside world to support their grandiose sense of self. For example, a grandiose narcissist may pursue power at all costs, even if it means harming innocent people, because it caters to their sense of omnipotence, garners admiration from others, and validates their excessive sense of entitlement, which can be very rewarding for them. In contrast, greater functional and structural connectivity between these brain regions has been associated with positive views of the self and higher self-esteem. However, this connection is a correlation and not necessarily a "cause" of their behavior. It's only one small piece of a larger puzzle and more studies need to be conducted on other factors involved.

Manipulation Tactics Narcissists and Psychopaths Use

You may have felt invalidated or doubted as a survivor of a toxic relationship with a narcissist. You could have wondered whether you were just "imagining" things or been accused of overreacting. People assume that when a partner is reporting on their psychopathic or narcissistic partner's traits, they must be exaggerating due to resentment or personal bias. In reality, as you learned, research shows that a loved one's assessment of narcissism in their partner actually tends to be highly correlated with expert assessments of narcissism, and it is far more accurate than how narcissists reported on their own traits and behaviors (e.g., Miller et al. 2005; Carlson et al. 2013). Another study shows that female participants actually tend to *underestimate* the psychopathic traits of their partners, which were also reported on by the partners themselves (Uzieblo et al. 2011).

Remember, the narcissist's ego needs mean they will present themselves in a distorted light to society, and their partner or loved one who experiences their behavior thus tends to be a more accurate reporter of their true traits and behaviors (e.g., Grijalva & Zhang 2016). This contradicts the assumption that survivors would be "exaggerating" the traits and behaviors of their partners and actually shows that the deception from psychopathic individuals may lead to survivors not even being aware of the full extent of how psychopathic their partners truly are. Bottom line?

If you're a survivor of a relationship with a psychopath or narcissist, it's very unlikely you are "exaggerating."

Thankfully, we have crucial data about the manipulation tactics narcissistic and psychopathic individuals use, and we also now have research studies to back up the association between these tactics and these traits. Learning more about their tactics can help remind you that you are not alone and that many survivors experience similar trials and tribulations. It is not your fault.

Gaslighting

Gaslighting is a manipulation tactic designed to distort your reality and make you question your perceptions, thoughts, and emotions. In my study's sample of survivors, 95 percent of survivors had experienced gaslighting, and this was true for those who had partners with narcissistic as well as psychopathic traits (Arabi 2023). Past researchers have also observed the link between gaslighting and psychopathic traits (e.g., Leedom et al. 2019).

Gaslighting can strengthen the trauma bond by causing you to see the narcissistic abuser as the arbiter of your reality. You become trained by them throughout the relationship to no longer trust your emotions, your beliefs, or yourself. You seek comfort from the abuser after abusive incidents because they have dictated that they are the only one who sees you and your circumstances accurately. In reality, they're handing you a funhouse mirror that distorts your self-perception, harming your self-esteem in agonizing ways.

Below, you will see examples of gaslighting from survivors who participated in my research study. Some details have been obscured to protect the anonymity of participants.

Examples of Gaslighting from Survivors

"Gradually, he gaslit me into believing that I was losing my mind. Early on, he would tell me I misheard him or misunderstood.

Later, he told me that I was overtired, "over-the-top," or paranoid. By the end, he flat out told me I was [crazy]. Meanwhile, he was doing crazy-making things like hiding things from me, changing things and telling me he hadn't, putting my things in strange places, telling people lies [about me]. It took me a long time when I was out of the relationship to realize that I was never crazy! He was intentionally trying to make me look nuts and go crazy!"

"If I asked why he hadn't even read my text for days, he'd say, 'You're crazy and possessive and I am just busy.' I didn't realize how he was the one being unreasonable. I started to believe I was insane and started to think I needed to be in therapy."

"Nothing is ever as serious as I think. Her affairs are never that serious, she can never 'remember' details about them. She will say things to me and completely deny she ever said them."

"He would regularly tell me that I was overreacting and was too emotional. I was never allowed to have feelings about anything. Even if I was agreeing with him! He'd tell me to calm down and give me looks like he was afraid of me, or say I was crazy. If I ever got passionate about a subject, he constantly accused me of the [negative] things that *he* was. I constantly struggled to try to prove myself (it was never enough) and started actually believing some of it."

"She would make me feel as if something was wrong with me mentally or that I am crazy whenever I was going through a situation that was bothering me emotionally. She would tell me to stop being obsessed about it and would completely dismiss it as utter nonsense to her. She would imply to me to just get over it and that's that. Total invalidation of what I was going through at the time. When she would pressure and coerce me into problematic situations, [...] she would play innocent and play the victim. She would act like everything was all my fault, all while completely absolving herself from the situation she initially started.

This left me confused and full of cognitive dissonance due to me being gaslit by focusing on my participation in the situation."

"He accused me of being paranoid and jealous when I would confront him about women he'd been seen with. Belittled me for my depression. Told me I was crazy. Repeatedly told me I was too sensitive and needed to toughen up."

"They have tried to paint me as the abuser, despite acknowledging their lies and violations of consent. They pushed me so far over the edge a few times that they have been able to point to my mental breakdowns as evidence of my unreliability."

"Constant lies about everything—where she was going, why she couldn't answer her phone for hours at a time, why she couldn't see me that day or the next. Pretty much everything aside from when we were physically together was fabricated for whatever reason. Sometimes she'd admit things, but only to use it against me later. She told pretty much everyone that I was delusional, and there was nothing between us, and we were never together, even though people saw us together kissing and being romantic."

"I have been told I am crazy, delusional, too sensitive, that 'it didn't happen like that.' He would turn the lights on and off and tell me he did not do it. He would have our child hide when I was looking for them, only to appear to call me crazy. When trying to question him, he would refuse to answer until I controlled my tone and kept saying it over and over until I gave up and was silent. He would keep me within the confines of the silent treatment for weeks."

"He would always claim he told me about something or experienced something with me that I could not recall. I'm now convinced those were lies designed to get me to question my own memory. Later, he would dismiss me anytime I remembered a fact that was contradictory to lies he was trying to sell me on and tell me I was remembering wrong and it didn't happen. I got to the point where I stopped questioning him because [I thought] I was probably forgetting something or remembering things wrong."

"He constantly gaslit me throughout the relationship. Telling me that I had a bad memory or that I can't remember anything or that something didn't happen when I knew it did."

"He had me locked up in a psychiatric hospital."

"He has often badgered me with descriptions of things he says I did that never happened. He would constantly say, 'That never happened, you must be crazy,' and that no one will believe me because he even admitted to going to [people] and telling [them] that I was the one trying to hurt him."

"I would ask him to do something [many] times and he would say, 'You never told me, you might think you did.' I would tell him what I [was] doing, I would tell him and he would ask me again, many times throughout the day. He would tell me that he didn't say or do the things he did. He would deny telling others what I heard or saw him saying online...until I showed him the screenshots. I had to record [his threats] to replay later to prove to myself that he said it because he would swear I was lying […] and imagining it all."

"If I was upset about something (say, him texting another woman while married to me) he would twist the conversation around, saying it was my fault that I don't trust him, until I was the one apologizing."

"She would and still manages to twist everything to suit herself and appear the victim. I had to start taking screenshots to have proof that I wasn't crazy. Even now she will text me things that never happened and try and convince me that they did. It's basically every single conversation."

"He would turn off lights and say he didn't. Say things he later denied. Every argument he would twist into my fault, and I would end up apologizing."

Jealousy Induction or Triangulation

Jealousy induction (or what is more colloquially known as romantic *triangulation*) is the act of purposely trying to provoke jealousy in someone, often by bringing the presence of someone into the dynamic of your relationship in explicit or implicit ways. In my study, 76 percent of survivors had experienced jealousy induction (Arabi 2023). According to past researchers, grandiose narcissists (who feel entitled, seek admiration, and believe in their superiority) provoked jealousy in their partners for the purposes of gaining power and control, while more vulnerable narcissists (who are more hypersensitive and anxious) induced jealousy not only to gain power and control, but also to exact revenge on the partner, test and strengthen the relationship, seek security, and compensate for low self-esteem (Tortoriello et al. 2017).

In another 2017 research study by Massar and colleagues, 347 individuals (both men and women) filled out measures on psychopathy, jealousy, and jealousy induction. This study found that people who exhibited the traits of primary psychopathy (associated with grandiosity and low anxiety and said to be "born" rather than made by their environment) tended to deliberately provoke jealousy to gain control over their partners and to exact revenge (for example, in cases where they felt jealous themselves).

Similar to vulnerable narcissists in the study by Tortoriello and colleagues, those who had the traits of secondary psychopathy (associated with criminal behaviors and impulsivity and thought to be shaped by their environment) also induced jealousy to gain power and control, but also did so to test the relationship and gain self-esteem. Interestingly, both primary and secondary psychopathy are associated with experiencing *emotional jealousy* (jealousy in response to a perceived threat), while secondary psychopathy is associated with both *emotional* and *suspicious jealousy* (jealousy that is preemptive and centered around concerns of infidelity as well as "checking" behaviors, such as going through their partner's belongings or text messages). This reveals that although psychopathic partners may repeatedly provoke jealousy in you, it's likely they are also experiencing jealousy and suspicions themselves.

By subjecting you to implicit or explicit comparisons, flaunting past partners or potential prospects, or constantly bringing others into the dynamic of the relationship, you become trained to "compete" for the narcissist, even if you were the one who was originally less interested in *them*. You also lose a sense of your uniqueness and positive qualities as you become hyperfocused on the love triangles they manufacture, and this takes a toll on your self-worth and self-perception over time. The narcissist skews your self-perception so you no longer see yourself and your positive qualities accurately and feel less important and valuable.

Examples of Jealousy Induction from Survivors

"He insisted on maintaining communication with so many of his past partners and ex-spouses. I am not the jealous type, but this was glaringly important to him, and not for the reasons he gave me."

"She would tell me it was hot when I got jealous and describe in great detail anytime she went out and got hit on. She would also text other women when her screen was slightly in my view."

"He flirted with everyone. Stared at women right in front of me. Talked about how many people want him. And always talked about past conquests and how many girls [pursued him] decades ago. He would do this whenever we were on a date. Constantly comparing me to others. I could barely get a word in."

"He had a 'special' relationship with his best friend, who was female… When we were separated, prior to the divorce, he slept with different women. He made a point to show off these women to our mutual friends."

"She constantly compared me to her exes in an attempt to ruin my self-esteem."

"He would say he was sleeping with the girl who I was suspicious about. He would text me things…and then 'sorry, wrong woman,' and it was on purpose. He would make up names of women that he said he was seeing and would create lies surrounding them just to try and make me jealous and make himself seem sought-after to make me want to come back to him."

"He would frequently tell me how women were hitting on him or complimenting him when he was out. He also became upset if I didn't get upset or jealous about this."

"He constantly tried to make me feel inferior by making little digs about [me], and even made up stuff and applied it to me. He would talk constantly about women at work."

"He sent me pictures that girls would send to him. He talked about his feelings for female coworkers."

"He constantly flirted and looked at women and men… He would take me around his hookups, which made us both uncomfortable but he'd deny anything."

"He was constantly comparing me to ex-lovers and coworkers. He was always looking at other people in a sexual manner and verbalized it to me."

"He bragged about how much women love him and want to be with him. How adorable they are and important to him. He showered them with physical attention right in front of me, but [not me]. Madonna/whore syndrome."

"He said if any man showed interest in me, it was only [sexual]… Meanwhile, he'd give me the silent treatment after I got all dressed up for him, and talk and flirt with other women in front of me when we went out anywhere."

"He was always talking to other women and touching them and hugging them in front of me. Usually, he never introduced me to them."

Love Bombing

Love bombing is a manipulation tactic that is often used in cults to groom new members. Cult leaders make members feel welcome, special, and adored so these members become bonded to the leaders and the group despite red flags and boundary-breaking behaviors. In a relationship with a narcissist, you often become part of a one-person cult where the narcissist showers you with constant praise and attention to win your loyalty. In my study, with a sample of 1,294 participants, 79 percent of survivors had experienced love bombing (Arabi 2023). In another study's sample of 484 college students, love bombing was associated with narcissistic tendencies and negatively correlated with self-esteem and the use of more media and texting in romantic relationships (Strutzenberg et al. 2017). Love bombing is usually accompanied by tactics such as mirroring and future faking—where the narcissist mirrors your interests, hobbies, and personality traits, or dangles the carrot of a future they don't intend to fulfill just to get you invested in them.

Love bombing centers you so you begin to center the narcissist and make them your entire world. They fixate on you and establish a connection with you, weaponizing excessive contact and attention. This sets the pathway for trauma bonding to begin, and conditions you to chase the narcissist in hopes of regaining the false future they once fed to you. In this phase, you are "locked in" to a cycle with a narcissist, tethered to the euphoric ways they make you feel. Many survivors note that love bombing was followed abruptly by devaluation after a key transition period where the survivor was sufficiently invested in the narcissist, such as marriage, pregnancy, or moving in together. You then reminisce about the joyful memories, the grand promises, and the false self the narcissist once presented after they began to devalue you. This can keep you stuck in the relationship as you experience cognitive dissonance about the false self they presented and their true self.

Examples of Love Bombing from Survivors

"He told me I was the most fascinating woman he had ever met. He adored me. Swept me off to Europe for my birthday. By the end, he was critical of everything I did."

"In the beginning she was so sweet. So loving, liked all the things I did. She said 'I love you' in the first week. Treated me like I was the woman of her dreams. As soon as I felt the same, allowed her to move in with me, and officially became her girlfriend, she [hit] me the first time."

"He was super nice and attentive at the beginning. He quickly moved in with me in a matter of weeks. We married quickly. That was when I realized that I couldn't go too deep or ask too much of him or it would be hell."

"There would be over a hundred text messages in a day from him. He would call me his wife from the beginning, the love of his life, brought whatever personal effects from home he could bring over 'as a gift.' I was expected to keep in constant contact."

"When we met, he would shower me with kind words, flowers, and gifts, telling me and the world how amazing and smart I was. Once we were married, this slowly changed until I got pregnant… He stopped being kind and started controlling every move."

"He was not my 'type' of man but swept me off my feet in the beginning. It happened so fast. I didn't understand at that time that I was being love bombed by a narcissist. He would then begin to use intermittent reinforcement by causing an argument, then disappearing for a while, before the abuse became a daily occurrence and I was a shell of my former self."

"He acted really supportive and sweet for years, then he withdrew any form of physical contact or affection after we got married."

Stonewalling

In a 2015 study by Horan and colleagues, individuals with personality traits such as narcissism, psychopathy, and Machiavellianism were shown to be more likely to use contempt, criticism, stonewalling, and defensiveness in their relationships. In the context of abusive relationships, *stonewalling* is a behavior in which a manipulator shuts down conversations, abruptly withdraws from conversations where they are being held accountable, and refuses to engage in a healthy dialogue about their behavior.

The term *Dark Triad* refers to these three dark personality traits, which share features of aggression, deception, and emotional insensitivity. Although these traits overlap in many ways, they can also be distinct from one another. Machiavellianism, for example, emphasizes the ability to be manipulative and cunning to meet one's needs no matter what to rise to power, which can overlap with some of the behaviors of narcissism and psychopathy. However, narcissism is more often characterized by grandiosity, while psychopathy also has thrill-seeking behaviors.

The behaviors associated with the Dark Triad personality traits are known as the Four Horsemen of the Apocalypse, which researchers associate with predicting the ending of a relationship (Gottman & Silver 1999). In my 2023 study, 93 percent of survivors had experienced stonewalling. Stonewalling can be part of a "demand-withdraw" pattern in relationships where victims attempt to resolve issues or confront the abuse, only to be shut down by their abusers, who then withdraw from them. These withdrawing behaviors may be processed by the brain as a form of romantic rejection, and such rejection can activate brain networks associated with loss, craving, and emotion regulation (Cacioppo & Cacioppo 2016). This makes stonewalling especially harmful to someone's mental health, especially if used chronically. Many survivors reported that stonewalling and the silent treatment were used as tactics to silence them when they were trying to hold their partners accountable for abusive behaviors and manipulation, eroding their boundaries. Stonewalling contributes to the trauma bond because you learn to chase after the abuser and silence yourself and your needs, rights, boundaries, and emotions. You abandon the respect and consideration you deserve.

Examples of Stonewalling from Survivors

"He would often stonewall me and constantly walked out when I confronted him. On a special occasion he left me in a foreign city all alone. Then, when I would get home, he'd tell me how women were hitting on him—to make me feel like it was my fault he left and it was probably a way of trying to manipulate me into not confronting his behaviors anymore."

"If he was told he did something that upset me, he'd turn it around and shut down the conversation. The silent treatment was often used to enforce his punishment for making him take accountability. The longest silent treatment was three months."

"I was always afraid to bring anything up because I knew it would start a big fight. Anytime I had the courage to bring it up, I would gently start with something small, like when he treated me so coldly after a fight. He would start off by telling me how sorry he was and that he would work on his temper, then when I would get to the bigger issues... He would really be upset and start shouting in anger...then he would either lock himself in the room or take off."

"The second any conversation wasn't going her way, she would avoid anything that was being brought up and instead tell me how everything is always my fault and how horrible I am and then refuse to discuss anything further. If I continued to push, she would tell me that we were broken up and that I needed to apologize to her for upsetting her."

"He gets loud and defensive if I try to discuss anything that bothers me in which he may have done something wrong. No matter my approach, how calm, even if I am just trying to discuss it. He screams and acts intimidating."

"I was constantly being given the silent treatment for doing the wrong things. If I didn't give the right answer to things he would decide to leave the house and spend all day gone with no explanation of where he went."

"If I started to bring anything up it was met with a passive-aggressive response of 'Of course it's my fault! It's always my fault! I will just go back to not saying anything.'"

"She would never admit she had ever done anything wrong. She denied and shut down any conversation regarding her behavior, blaming everyone else around her."

"He would read the message asking him to explain his behavior or even asking what was going on between us. Then he would ignore me, totally forget me for a whole day. Then message me back and not acknowledge anything."

"He never acknowledged being wrong, never apologized to me for being hurtful. Anytime I tried to talk to him about his inappropriate behavior he would belittle me or tell me I was crazy, that he didn't do that type of behavior."

"The first time I confronted him about lying he denied it, fabricated more stories, and then told me I needed to leave because he didn't want to have a bad night with me."

Malicious Envy

Benign envy is envy that inspires positive action—like improving oneself or setting goals. *Malicious envy* is envy that can drive actions to sabotage, harm, or inflict injury on the reputation of another person. In multiple studies with a total of 3,123 participants, Lange and colleagues (2018) investigated whether benign or malicious envy was associated with

Dark Triad personality traits. They found that while benign envy was associated with more Machiavellian behaviors, malicious envy was associated with both psychopathic and Machiavellian behaviors. Lange and colleagues also identified that malicious envy is related to vulnerable narcissism and narcissistic rivalry, an antagonistic facet of narcissism discussed in another 2016 study. For example, many survivors I have spoken to have noted that narcissistic people tried to sabotage them at their workplace if they were envious of their skill sets and talents, or tried to derail their careers to have more power over them. They did this by misrepresenting their actions to their superiors, engaging in covert and underhanded bullying to try to punish them for doing well and outshining their peers, or taking away privileges or resources that would help them move up the corporate ladder.

In the context of romantic relationships, survivors have shared how their narcissistic partners started arguments before important interviews, meetings, and presentations, or coerced them into quitting jobs or halting their education to rely on them for an income, only to financially abuse them. Some survivors have even been reproductively abused during the high points of their careers, as their partners interfered with their birth control to ensure they would lose years of work so they could "stay home with the kids."

You can find guided meditations to begin to heal from the effects of gaslighting, stonewalling, and pathological envy at http://www.newhar binger.com/53561.

Similarities and Differences Between Narcissism and Psychopathy

You may be wondering, if both narcissists and psychopaths use the same manipulation tactics, then why should it matter whether they are a narcissist or a psychopath? It's true that we should be addressing the overlaps. But, as you learned, there are some key similarities and differences to keep in mind because they could affect your well-being and safety. Here is a summary and additional information comparing these personalities.

Understanding these differences will also allow you to customize your strategies for defending and protecting yourself, as we'll discuss more in chapter 4.

Narcissists have a more prominent need for external validation. Narcissistic personality disorder and narcissistic traits are characterized by a desire for and entitlement to validation from the world and an inflated sense of self-importance. As you learned earlier, narcissists excessively demand attention, praise, and adoration from others. Psychopaths have impoverished emotions and more callous-unemotional traits; they can appear cold and unfeeling to the opinions of others. Unless someone's perspective affects their personal agenda to seek profit or pleasure, they typically don't need as much external validation.

This is important to keep in mind because if you need to enforce boundaries with a narcissist or require cooperation from them (for example, in cases of co-parenting), you will likely need to appeal to their ego and sense of self (e.g., telling them they will be Dad of the Year if they take their children to the amusement park during their scheduled visitation), whereas if you're dealing with someone who doesn't require as much validation, you may need to appeal to their need for profit or pleasure (e.g., letting a psychopathic coworker know the immense profits a certain project you need approved will bring in). You can find more tips for how to deal with a narcissist or psychopath you can't avoid in chapter 5.

Narcissists lack empathy, but psychopaths lack remorse. While both can harm others with their aggression, the psychopath is usually more dangerous because they have less holding them back. Psychopaths are lacking not only empathy but also remorse. This is what makes them especially conscienceless in their transgressions toward others. As mentioned previously, numerous fMRI studies reveal that psychopaths have differences in their brains that may affect their moral sensitivity, feelings of fear, and sense of guilt (Harenski et al. 2010; Deming et al. 2020; Gong et al. 2019). Past studies have shown reduced gray matter in areas of the brain such as the prefrontal cortex and the limbic system (Ermer et al. 2012; Koenigs 2012). Thus, psychopaths are less inhibited and don't have much holding them back from committing even the most sadistic crimes imaginable. Vulnerable narcissists might experience more shame, especially if they are outed for their true character in the public eye, but grandiose narcissists may take pride in committing horrific crimes even when they are exposed. If you suspect you're with a psychopathic person, you will likely need to do more careful safety planning as you strategize how to exit the relationship and avoid any and all in-person contact in the event of a breakup, for example.

Narcissists and psychopaths both use their keen understanding of human nature and "cognitive empathy" to manipulate others. Both narcissists and psychopaths possess cognitive empathy—the ability to understand and identify the emotions of others. Studies show that they intellectually know the difference between right and wrong, but they lack affective empathy, the ability and willingness to care about the emotions of others (Cima, Tonnaer, & Hauser 2010). Some narcissistic and psychopathic individuals sadistically enjoy toying with and deliberately causing pain to others. This is known as *duping delight*, and studies show it's associated with psychopathic traits. This gives them a grandiose sense of power and control and a smug sense of satisfaction that they have "one-upped" you with their perpetual cat-and-mouse games.

Reactive and premeditated aggression are found in both. These two pathological personalities can engage in multiple forms of aggression, including reactive and proactive (premeditated) aggression. Narcissistic reactive rage is called *narcissistic rage* in response to perceived slights, but it can also be premeditated as well. For example, a narcissist may go out of their way in a calculated fashion to sabotage or harm someone they know is surpassing them at work. Psychopaths can be violently reactive in their aggression (more likely with impulsive, secondary psychopaths), yet primary, low-anxious psychopaths are also very prone to instrumental aggression to achieve a specific purpose (such as conning others for pleasure or profit). Use this knowledge to avoid sharing your achievements or upcoming projects with envious individuals who may try to sabotage them. Always avoid in-person contact or bring a witness if you are communicating a boundary with someone you perceive to be dangerous.

Malicious envy is present in both narcissists and psychopaths. Narcissists and psychopaths can both experience malicious envy, where they go out of their way to lash out and target others. There may be subtle differences in why and how they lash out based on the particular type of narcissism and psychopathy involved (Lange, Paulhus, & Crusius 2018; Lange, Crusius, & Hagemeyer 2016). Grandiose narcissists and psychopaths are more similar in their predilections because they genuinely believe they are superior to others and entitled to violate others for their own gain—even going so far as to steal the work of others and profit off their labor while taking credit. Research by Papageorgiou and colleagues (2019) indicates that for narcissists who have grandiose traits, these traits can protect them against stress or depression. They may be more likely to lash out or use rage as a control tactic when their sense of superiority and excessive sense of entitlement are challenged; studies show they display more physiological stress responses when presented with an "ego threat" (Jauk & Kanske 2021).

As you better understand the sources of malicious envy in your narcissistic or psychopathic partner's life, you can resist internalizing their attempts to deflate you or make you feel small and "translate" these attempts into how they reflect your strengths. For example, if your narcissistic partner always puts down your job, you can translate this into, "They are envious of my career and how well I am doing," rather than believing that their put-downs have any accuracy.

Psychopaths exhibit what researchers call a manufactured type of *cold rage*. According to Dr. Robert Hare, this is distinct from a "hair-trigger" hot-blooded rage that is more impulsive and spurred on by the heat of the moment. There is not much genuine emotion behind it; it is used solely to dominate and silence their victims. However, more vulnerable narcissists and those with the secondary subtype of psychopathy (known colloquially as the criminally inclined "sociopath") can battle self-esteem issues. Vulnerable narcissists who are more anxious and defensive and secondary psychopaths also lash out in rage, but they may be more likely than grandiose narcissists and primary psychopaths to be battling a sense of inferiority when doing so. Regardless of their subtype, such rage and aggression are inexcusable and cause irreparable harm.

Narcissism can be influenced by parental overvaluation and be partly hereditary as well. Primary psychopaths can be biologically predisposed to psychopathy, but secondary psychopaths are more influenced by their childhood environment. As noted before, longitudinal research suggests that parental overvaluation—such as spoiling and coddling a child—predicts narcissistic traits more than lack of parental warmth or parental maltreatment. The secondary subtype of psychopathy is more associated with childhood trauma, while the primary psychopath ("born rather than made") is less likely to report childhood trauma or post-traumatic stress symptoms. Narcissism is also a moderately heritable trait. Knowing this can help you avoid overly rationalizing a narcissist's or psychopath's behavior as you break free from trauma bonds because you understand that their behavior cannot be attributed to their childhood alone and the fact that they are continuing to *choose* to engage in these behaviors.

Both narcissists and psychopaths can manufacture chaos on purpose. However, people with a higher level of psychopathic traits may find it especially rewarding because they need constant stimulation and are prone to boredom. According to expert Dr. Robert Hare's psychopathy checklist, psychopaths are prone to boredom and require constant stimulation. Psychopaths are high-sensation seekers and often go too far in their search for a thrill, engaging in reckless or impulsive behavior that harms themselves or others. Paired with their deficiencies in fear, this makes for a dangerous combination.

Neuroscience studies by Buckholtz and colleagues (2010) point to the psychopath's hyperactive dopamine system and subsequent need to obtain a reward at all costs to explain their impulsive, reckless, and harmful behavior. However, earlier research by Gerra and colleagues (2003) shows reduced dopaminergic receptor sensitivity in psychopaths, suggesting that some psychopaths may actually be *less* responsive to dopamine and therefore require more of an intense thrill to get a sense of reward. While more studies are needed on psychopathy and dopamine, it's clear that a psychopath's dysfunctional reward system can affect their constant need for stimulation. When you observe a psychopath abruptly devalue you while suddenly love bombing another victim, or becoming laser-focused on a new target, or engaging in high-risk activities, understand that this is part of their thrill-seeking behavior and propensity for boredom: it has nothing whatsoever to do with you or your worth, and has everything to do with their own choices.

Narcissists may be less willing to engage in risk and have more limits and constraints on what they're willing to do to meet their needs because they are focused on maintaining their status and reputation. They tend to have more fear than the more "fearless" psychopath. Not only are narcissists more worried about incurring harm to their own well-being, but they are also concerned with "looking" good and propping up their self-image. If you have been devalued by a narcissistic individual, understand that your ability to discern their true self threatens their ego, which is why they must pursue a new target to prop up their image once more, only to repeat the vicious cycle with all their victims.

Narcissists care about their reputation. Psychopaths (especially the secondary, impulsive subtype) can engage in more reckless and impulsive behavior, violating laws and the rights of others. Both narcissists and psychopaths can be superficially charming. For narcissists, this charm is utilized to facilitate relationships that give the narcissist valuable "narcissistic supply," such as attention, praise, and validation. For psychopaths, their superficial and glib charm is one of the most potent ways they are able to con and exploit others for resources. For example, people duped by the psychopath may find themselves handing over loans or their savings because they "seemed so sincere." If you have been a victim of a psychopath's or narcissist's charisma and charm, or have fallen prey to their cons, don't blame yourself. Even psychopathy experts like Dr. Robert Hare admit to being duped.

As we've touched on before, psychopaths who fit the more impulsive secondary subtype often have an extensive criminal history or at the very least a marked history of violating the rights of others. The most extreme psychopaths could even have murder, robbery, or strangulation in their records. Low-anxious psychopaths may evade consequences more easily or commit crimes they can get away with—perhaps they embezzle funds from the companies they work for or regularly commit sexual assault but use their charisma and connections to escape responsibility and legal consequences. They could be parasitic and leech off of vulnerable people without it being considered "illegal." For example, a romantic partner with psychopathic traits might love bomb a partner into providing for him. These types know how to fly under the radar. It's important to understand this as you reflect on your own relationship with a psychopathic or narcissistic individual.

Narcissists may or may not have been involved in criminal activity and tend to engage in more emotional and psychological forms of con artistry. Due to their desire to maintain a stellar reputation, they may avoid too many risky behaviors that could expose them. Yet both narcissists and psychopaths can live double lives. Remember, narcissists tend to engage in impression management and wear a convincing false mask so they look like a good person to others. They may be restrained by their self-image, whereas psychopaths don't care as much about their reputation or status, although they may attempt to maintain their reputation if they feel they can gain something from it. If you are thinking of seeking justice or accountability during any part of your healing journey, it can help to keep this in mind so you can carefully avoid their retaliation, evaluate your specific situation with both the potential risks and consequences as well as benefits involved, and gather as much evidence and witnesses as possible if you do move forward.

Both narcissists and psychopaths do not fare well in therapy. Research indicates that psychopaths can actually sharpen their manipulation tools in therapy and have a high recidivism rate if they are criminals. It's never advisable to take a narcissist to couples therapy, as this is a primary site for them to further gaslight and traumatize their victims. Younger individuals with antisocial or psychopathic traits who bully others, commit crimes, and show cruelty to animals may benefit from contingency-management programs that reward prosocial behaviors while discouraging harm toward others, although underlying callous-unemotional traits (which are genetically influenced) are unlikely to change.

However, for adult psychopaths, therapy can actually heighten the risk of their harm to society. A review of the research by Anderson and Kiehl (2014) actually shows that psychopathic individuals tend to get even *more* manipulative in therapy by learning how to mimic empathy and better understand how to tap into the vulnerabilities of others. This exacerbating effect of treatment is important to consider as studies reveal that psychopaths tend to have a high recidivism rate and are five times more likely than nonpsychopathic offenders to reoffend violently (Reidy, Kearns, & DeGue 2013). If you are hanging on to the false hope that therapy will change the psychopathic person in your life, you must understand that there is a high risk that therapy can actually worsen their manipulation tactics.

Practically speaking, it may not matter whether you're dealing with a narcissist or a psychopath if the harm that is done to you is immense. However, psychopaths are capable of sadistic violence without as many limits as narcissists. If you do notice psychopathic traits in a partner, it can be helpful to see this as an extra risk factor and take safety precautions ahead of time.

The following chart summarizes many of the differences and similarities noted above. Do note that while narcissists may not have the same features as psychopaths, some narcissists may still have some traits and behaviors, which is why those items are left blank—to account for the possibility of those traits and behaviors being present, rather than indicating they definitely won't possess those traits and behaviors. You can also download this chart at http://www.newharbinger.com/53561.

Narcissism and Psychopathy Checklist

Behaviors and Traits	Narcissism	Psychopathy
Lack of empathy	☑	☑
Lack of remorse		☑
Parasitic lifestyle		☑
Superficial charm	☑	☑
Thrill-seeking; prone to boredom and high sensation-seeking		☑
Need for attention and admiration	☑	
Aggressive and bullying behaviors, both covert and overt	☑	☑
Sadistic, gratuitous violence		☑
Breaks the law and usually has a history of doing so		☑
Malicious envy and sabotage of others	☑	☑
Becomes more manipulative in therapy	☑	☑
Provokes jealousy for power and control, to exact revenge, or to test relationship	☑	☑
Engages in both reactive and premeditated aggression to achieve goals	☑	☑
Weaponizes cognitive empathy to assess someone's emotions to manipulate them	☑	☑
Can be shaped by parental overvaluation in childhood but also has a hereditary component	☑	
Has a primary subtype that reports less childhood trauma and is more likely to be biologically predisposed		☑

Takeaways

In this chapter, you learned about the differences between the various types of narcissism and psychopathy, including grandiose narcissism and vulnerable narcissism, as well as between primary and secondary psychopathy, understanding their traits and aggressive behaviors such as gaslighting, love bombing, and jealousy induction on a deeper level. You now have a better understanding of the ways people with dark personality traits can manipulate you in relationships, as well as how their brains work differently, often lacking in empathy and, in cases of psychopathy, lacking fear of consequences. You may feel yourself waking up and realizing that you, too, experienced these tactics.

You might feel overwhelmed, knowing this manipulation was deliberate and that people who repeat harmful behavior may never change. Be gentle with yourself and know that you can use this knowledge to empower yourself whenever you deal with a toxic person or encounter a manipulator. You can now adjust your own behavior, depending on the type of dark personality traits you are dealing with, toward boundaries, self-care, and seeking safety. You can now detach from the toxicity of the relationship, with full knowledge of the other person's aims rather than rationalizing their motives or minimizing the harm they do.

In the next chapter, you will learn more about the trauma bonds that keep you attached to these types.

CHAPTER 3

Understanding the
Trauma Bond

You've learned in depth about how these types of personalities work. Now let's circle back to how they manufacture strong trauma bonds with their victims. It can be very difficult to deal with a dark, manipulative personality—one who lacks empathy for your emotions and needs, throws you under the bus after you've invested so much into the relationship, and is callous about the way they mistreat you after setting up false promises and expectations through love bombing. The trauma bond can be brutal and filled with mixed emotions, so if you've made it this far in the book to help you better understand why manipulative individuals treat you this way, you are very strong. You might still have many questions about why it is so hard to leave such a toxic relationship.

According to researchers Reid and colleagues (2013), in order to survive the abusive environment, the trauma bond makes you engage in behaviors to appease your partner in an attempt to avoid further abuse, mistreatment, or violence. You may even develop a sense of gratitude for being "allowed" to survive and given small mercies or minor acts of kindness because you've been gradually conditioned to accept less than the bare minimum as a form of control. A review of the research on trauma bonding in the context of sex trafficking by Casassa and colleagues (2022) indicates that the features of trauma bonding include the following:

- An imbalance of power that is disproportionately given to the perpetrator

- The perpetrator's intentional use of both positive and negative interactions with the victim

- The victim's gratitude for these positive interactions or small acts of kindness as well as self-blame

- The victim's internalization of the perpetrator's perspectives

- The past trauma of victims makes them more vulnerable and susceptible to trauma bonding

- The love that victims had for their abusers and traffickers remains even after they exit these situations, and tends to be one of the main reasons they don't prosecute

- Perpetrators intentionally cultivate this trauma bond presumably to maintain control and protect themselves

Those who are trauma bonded find themselves biochemically and psychologically attached to the abuser in ways that make it difficult to leave the relationship. Trauma bonding can cause you to tolerate escalating mistreatment because you are forced to stay focused on survival. You may rationalize increasingly toxic behaviors, maintaining the relationship because you feel unable to protect yourself otherwise. You may even develop the need to defend and protect your abuser to your family members, friends, and even law enforcement.

It's important to remember that trauma bonding has little to do with the actual merits of the abuser or how "strong" you are. So if you're blaming yourself for staying, or find yourself romanticizing your abuser, know that this is just a common effect of the abuse you've experienced. Even the strongest of people can become trauma bonded to an abuser who has subjected them to chronically cruel and callous treatment. Due to their lack of empathy and ability to manipulate, deceive, gaslight, and subject you to countless mind games, narcissistic and psychopathic individuals specifically create very powerful trauma bonds with their partners. You are not alone, and you are doing what you can to survive. You should be proud of yourself for how far you've come.

The Neuroscience of Trauma Bonding

Why is it so difficult to detach ourselves from trauma bonds? As you learned in chapter 1, the trauma of the emotionally abusive relationship has effects on your brain. There is a reason why the manipulation tactics narcissists and psychopaths use to tether you to them work so effectively to tie you to them biochemically. Here are some of the ways these manipulation tactics strengthen the way your brain responds to the trauma bond.

Intermittent Reinforcement

A powerful way narcissistic individuals establish trauma bonds with their victims is through a method known as *intermittent reinforcement*. This is also a key stage in the trauma-bonding cycle, which we'll explore in a later section of this chapter. When using intermittent reinforcement, they will blow hot and cold, vacillating between tenderness and torment to get you fixated on them and seeking their validation—you are always chasing the next "fix" or "reward" that is their rare moments of kindness. They'll incorporate unpredictably timed displays of affection and attention into the abuse cycle so that you never know what version of them you're going to get next. They may love bomb you with excessive praise one minute, only to abruptly withdraw and emotionally withhold from you, treating you with cruelty and contempt. They may shower you with affection one day, only to give you the silent treatment the next.

In the beginning, they'll be very alluring with their false charismatic mask, only to pull the rug up from under you with callous indifference and devaluation that make you doubt yourself. If you're wondering whether that's deliberate, it is. It can give narcissists a sense of power that they have so much control over your emotions and that you will work harder to please them even as they mistreat you.

You may wonder, why would you feel so addicted and crave approval from the very person who mistreats you? It's because our brains can unfortunately be rewired by tactics like intermittent reinforcement to fixate on toxic people. Fisher and colleagues (2016) conducted research that illustrates that people in adverse-ridden or unrequited relationships actually show activation in the same areas of the brain's reward system as people addicted to cocaine and other drugs. When narcissists or psychopaths subject you to a "mean and sweet" cycle of abuse, it's not unlike a destructive drug addiction with severe and painful withdrawal symptoms. It doesn't help that dopamine is also released during sexual activity, which reinforces this bond. Dopamine "cross-talks" with oxytocin to intensify attachment (more on dopamine and oxytocin below).

If everyone's brain releases dopamine and oxytocin when they are having a pleasurable encounter with their partner, then how does the brain operate differently when one is with a narcissistic or psychopathic partner? It's because of the *intermittent* nature of the reward. Research conducted by Zald and colleagues (2010) reveals that dopamine flows more readily in the brain when the perceived rewards are intermittent or given on an unpredictable schedule, causing you to engage in a behavior more intensely when you don't know when that reward will come. This unpredictable schedule of rewards establishes what Fisher (2016) calls the "frustration-attraction" experience that can become so addictive. As the narcissist's attention becomes more scarce, you increase your frantic attempts to regain the love-bombing stage of the relationship. Intermittent reinforcement can therefore create an even stronger attachment to a toxic partner.

Similar to a gambler at a slot machine who incurs major losses, you're conditioned to continue playing and investing in hopes of the elusive win. This is what is known in the economics world as the *sunk-cost fallacy*— continuing to invest in something because you perceive that your investment is too big to give up now. Yet instead of accepting these losses and moving on, you continue with the hope that there will be some compensation and a positive return for all the pain you've experienced.

Dopamine

Memorable and pleasurable experiences like romantic dates, excessive affection and attention, flattery, steamy sex, gifts, and grand romantic gestures can all release dopamine in the brain. Considering the way narcissists and psychopaths love bomb their partners, this can lead to dangerous waters. Dopamine is a neurotransmitter that helps activate brain pathways related to rewarding behaviors. Such behaviors don't always have a biological function, like eating or mating, and some of these rewards can be subjective to the individual and specific to the context. This generates automatic associations in the brain that link our romantic partners with a kind of "wanting" and craving desire and even associate our partners with our survival.

Dopamine also directs key areas of the brain's reward system, such as the ventral tegmental area, which affects pleasure and guides focused attention on obtaining awards, to communicate with other parts of the brain, like the striatum, prefrontal cortex, nucleus accumbens, caudate nucleus, amygdala, and hippocampus, that play a key role in habit formation, reward detection, action preparation, decision making, motor functions, memory, pleasure, and emotion (Shih et al. 2022; Baik 2020; Seshadri 2016; Earp et al. 2017; Fisher, Aron, & Brown 2006). This is how the brain remembers, for example, the pleasure and euphoria of a first kiss—how it "records" the movement of leaning forward toward a lover, and how it captures the emotion of joy when lips first meet. Such rewarding behaviors are encoded in the brain as pleasurable and memorable, and dopamine helps tell the brain to decide that we must "do it again."

Basically, dopamine tells our brain that we should engage in that behavior again to get that perceived reward. Through releasing dopamine, the brain learns and stores crucial information needed to get that reward and the cues associated with it. This way, the brain can alert you to the anticipation of the reward. Although dopamine is primarily about motivation and taking action to achieve a reward, the pleasure or intensity of an event also plays a role in releasing dopamine, and an abuser's use of love bombing and devaluation can fuel intensity and craving. Much like how drugs can hijack the brain into vicious cycles of addiction, your brain in love can become hijacked into destructive habits in toxic love, reducing judgment and fear and causing you to be more reckless in your evaluation of your partner.

It's important to note that for dopamine, researchers have discovered that *wanting* may be different from *liking*; the sensation of liking appears to be concentrated in certain hedonic hot spots in the brain in animal studies (Castro & Berridge 2017). You may feel especially motivated or "want" and crave pursuing your toxic partner to gain a potential reward, but not actually "like" or enjoy this activity in the long term the way you would enjoy a sweet dessert, especially when you know it's harmful to you. This is similar to how a person may not "like" gambling, excessive shopping, or other addictions, but still crave such activities and engage in compulsive habits to obtain a *perceived* reward.

Oxytocin

Oxytocin, known as the famous "cuddle" or love hormone, actually has a variety of different functions, including promoting trust, bonding, empathy, and cooperation (Zak, Kurzban, & Matzner 2005). It's released when we fall in love and during close physical contact, such as hugging, sex, labor, and breastfeeding. Some studies indicate that more oxytocin can promote trust levels; given this finding, this may affect the ways we bond with toxic partners even when they betray us due to our physical attachment to them. Oxytocin also plays a role in anxiety reduction and anti-stress functions (Takayanagi & Onaka 2021). Oxytocin is released during a variety of situations involving social stress, physiological stress (such as running), and relational distress—so you're not only getting a boost of oxytocin when you're physically affectionate with a narcissist but also when you are *stressed* by them.

Yet oxytocin can also promote bonding. This is important to remember because you may bond to a narcissist or psychopath especially during "hurt-and-rescue" methods, where they inflict pain, only to condition you to seek them out for comfort and validation. Oxytocin doesn't just bond you to healthy partners—it promotes and strengthens unhealthy attachments as well.

Oxytocin plays a role in abusers as well. Interestingly, research by DeWall and colleagues (2014) reveals that although oxytocin tends to increase prosocial behavior, it actually has the *opposite effect* in partners already prone to physical aggression. In aggressive people, it actually heightens their propensity toward aggression and intimate partner violence. This means despite a boost of oxytocin from physical affection bonding you to your abuser, the abuser "bonds" with you through heightened aggression and abuse. As the researchers note, "Among highly aggressive people, a boost of oxytocin may cause them to use aggression toward close others as a means of maintaining their relationship." Of course, this is no excuse for their behavior, but rather a way of understanding how an abuser's brain can work differently than yours, and to remind you of the potential dangers.

Serotonin

Serotonin is a neurotransmitter that is vital to the health of major organ systems and the central nervous system, and is a key driver behind our mood, willpower, and motivation. It plays an important role in almost all brain functions and is involved in many different mental health conditions. The density of serotonin transporters can be lower when we fall in love, undistinguishable from the serotonin transporter levels in people with obsessive-compulsive disorder (OCD), although there may be some gender differences (Marazziti et al. 1999; Marazziti & Stahl 2018; Langeslag et al. 2012). Yet despite these gender differences, the majority of both men and women in love tend to spend an immense amount of time preoccupied with their love interest. Low serotonin may contribute to our preoccupation or fixation with the narcissist or psychopath, intensifying the trauma bond.

Cortisol

Cortisol is our body's main stress hormone. Levels of cortisol can increase due to stress and can cause inflammation in the body. Studies show mixed results on whether cortisol levels are higher for those in love, but it's said that when levels of cortisol naturally rise in response to a romantic connection, it can create an intense preoccupation with our partners, as if our body is being alerted to a perceived emergency (Marazziti & Canale 2004; Weisman et al. 2014; Sorokowski et al. 2019). Interestingly, male narcissists tend to exhibit higher cortisol levels, which may be connected to their lower need for relationship commitment and higher levels of arousal and reactivity even to neutral situations (Reinhardt et al. 2012). On the survivor's side, what we can be sure of is that chronic stress, such as the stress of an abusive relationship, can also cause cumulative damage to the body by overwhelming what is known as our "allostatic load," the culmination of our stress and life events, which can lead to undesirable health outcomes (Guidi et al. 2021). Cortisol affects our insulin levels, which can affect weight gain. In some survivors, this can lead to heightened issues with body image, self-esteem, and even body dysmorphia, given that narcissists and psychopaths tend to hypercriticize the appearance of their partners during the devaluation phase.

The Stages of Trauma Bonding

Now that you know how addictive toxic cycles with abusive narcissists and psychopaths can be, let's talk more about how they keep you trapped in these cycles of manipulation by looking at the stages of trauma bonding. The stages of trauma bonding can be more cyclical than linear, but usually the first stage includes *love bombing* and *idealization* to cultivate your dependency. Next, there tends to be *cognitive dissonance* as the first incidents or "micro-betrayals" of abuse occur: you become confused and disoriented about the true nature of your partner, who appears to exhibit aggressive or manipulative traits and behaviors that seem out of character based on the way they depicted themselves in the beginning.

Then there is usually a stage that includes *intermittent reinforcement* of behaviors in which the narcissist appears to revert back to positive and loving behaviors but still incorporates cruelty to keep you off-kilter, making the relationship traumatic and unpredictable. These incidents escalate to the next stage known as *devaluation and identity erosion*, where the narcissist begins to degrade your perceptions, emotions, and positive qualities in order to keep you under their control. Closely linked with this devaluation is a feeling of becoming enmeshed with the narcissist's identity and even taking on some of their traits in order to survive the tumultuous relationship. You feel as if you are being erased as a person and your identity becomes a melting pot of survival strategies, maladaptive defense mechanisms, and harmful coping methods to maintain the relationship.

The trauma bond deepens if the relationship continues, and leads to the final phase: a sense of *learned helplessness* and *dangerous adaptation* to the toxicity of the abuse cycle, which often begins again as the abuser love bombs you when you make attempts to leave. Let's look at these stages in more detail.

Love Bombing and Idealization

In the beginning of a relationship with a narcissist, they mirror your interests, hobbies, goals, mannerisms, and personality traits to get you to believe that you are their "soulmate." They flatter and praise you excessively and engage in grand romantic gestures, such as offering you lavish gifts, flowers, and vacations. They future-fake you into believing they want marriage and children with you. This type of love bombing can be a powerful tool to weaponize against anyone who has experienced trauma or is seeking to fill a void, as mirroring and love bombing cultivate dependency, allowing the abuser to control you and exploit you. Dopamine and oxytocin are very prominent players in this stage of the abuse cycle, creating an intensely pleasurable attachment, while cortisol may rise to heighten this preoccupation and fixation on the toxic partner.

In my study, the majority of survivors at this early stage of trauma bonding noticed that narcissists fast-forwarded milestones of the relationship by moving in together quickly, getting engaged or married, and having children (Arabi 2023). Even for survivors whose relationship progressed at a slower pace, they experienced excessive communication and contact from the narcissist that created a reliance on their approval and constant praise. Survivors at this stage may or may not notice a red flag or two that anything is amiss, but they are more likely to rationalize it because the mask portrayed by the narcissist is convincing and compelling—and their "love" is all-consuming.

Cognitive Dissonance

In this stage, the narcissist creates cognitive dissonance by testing and violating your boundaries with increasing escalation. They will subject you to what I like to call *micro-betrayals*. These are the seemingly minor psychological "assaults" they use to create doubt in you. Many of these micro-betrayals are wielded with plausible deniability, so you're not sure whether they intentionally meant to harm you. For example, they may take a day to respond to a text when they would otherwise respond right away—a kind of micro "abandonment" before they start abandoning you in more blatant ways—or they may lash out with a subtly insulting remark where they would usually praise you. This gives you emotional whiplash as you begin to witness the cracks in their false mask.

Next, they may up the ante, perhaps disappearing during a time they're usually available. They might even do this during an important period of time—like when you're sick or when you've expressed you need to hear from them. You're shocked because you have not yet been devalued by the narcissist and are accustomed to their consistency. Whether it's leaving you on "read" or failing to be there for you, they'll return with an excuse that you'll be tempted to believe—if only because this is the "first" of many more disappearances to come.

After a period where the narcissist appeared to celebrate your accomplishments, they may start incorporating insidious comments that deflate your joy, project their own insecurities, rage in envy, compare you to others, fearmonger, or find supposed shortcomings. For example, if you tell them about how your boss complimented your project, they might call you a "show-off," which is abruptly distinct from their previous behavior of giving you healthy and consistent praise. These types of comments steadily become more antagonistic and distant or fail to acknowledge your achievements altogether. While these types of reactions may start out slowly in toxic relationships, the increasingly critical comments grow over time until it becomes apparent that the narcissist does not support you no matter what you achieve.

While there's nothing minor about gaslighting, the first time it happens may evade your notice. The narcissist or psychopath might pretend they didn't say something they actually did or make a comment that "teasingly" insults you or accuses you of something you didn't do. When you call it out, they may hide their true motives by pretending they didn't mean anything by it. You may feel momentarily disoriented and confused, yet you're willing to believe them because they provide a rationale for their behavior. Yet this micro-betrayal is just one of many to come. By testing you with these "minor" cruel comments disguised as jokes or denials about reality, they are figuring out how far they can go to pull the wool over your eyes. That way, you'll be "properly" desensitized to cruelty by the time they engage in more impactful gaslighting.

You may also experience the narcissist trying to evoke jealousy in you during this stage by bringing up their ex or other romantic suitors. They will then gaslight you into believing you misunderstood them or that they didn't do or say something they actually did. They will push your buttons in escalating fashion, trying to get you to react as you scramble to win back their approval. Unbeknownst to you, the narcissist follows this stage with every one of their victims and there is not much you can do to prevent them from breaking you down.

Intermittent Reinforcement

As we discussed above, intermittent reinforcement is how the abuser manufactures an addiction in you to pursue the relationship at all costs, even when it is harming you. Whether it's buying you flowers after an argument or being kinder than usual on a day you're waiting for them to snap at you, the narcissist creates an atmosphere of toxicity and unpredictability. You may start to fight back during this stage or become more compliant. The narcissist begins to mix mistreatment with love bombing in unpredictable ways, causing you to become fixated on them. They sneak in small acts of kindness to make their positive side seem more magnified in your eyes, so you feel grateful to have any kindness at all. As you learned, this will create the addictive "dopamine rush" of trying to reobtain some level of attention from the narcissist as the cycle starts to become more and more unpredictable. Dopamine is a major player in creating this kind of addiction because it flows more readily in the brain when the "rewards" are unpredictable and random—you have no way of knowing when the narcissist will be kind or cruel next, but you strengthen your efforts to please them and bend over backward to meet their needs.

Just as a person who takes you hostage might "reward" you, the prisoner, with food or the absence of physical punishment, you are taught that you must be "grateful" for the ability to survive at all. Gratitude acts as a survival mechanism, alerting you to resources that keep you alive. In a psychologically abusive relationship, you'll find ways to cope with the cruelty of a partner by remembering positive moments, or you might feel struck by "abuse amnesia"—gaps in memory that can cause you to gloss over the abusive incidents so you stay focused on survival. For example, you may momentarily "forget" or feel disassociated from the events of a day packed with abuse because your brain is trying to protect you, or you may choose to only focus on the positive moments of the day to maintain your reasons for staying in the relationship, please your abuser, and survive the turmoil.

Devaluation and Identity Erosion

This stage of the trauma bond is usually the most agonizing for survivors to endure as the narcissist hypercriticizes, nitpicks, and isolates you. Criticism becomes the narcissist's primary mode of communication as they stonewall, compare you to others, and subject you to the silent treatment. They neglect you and spread rumors about you to isolate you from friends or family (or pit you against your loved ones). As a result, you begin to withdraw from your usual activities and social life as self-isolation becomes your new normal.

The narcissist also starts to weaponize hurt-and-rescue methods to keep you coming back to them to seek comfort and validation after abusive incidents. For example, they may set up a scenario where they call you a hurtful name under the guise of a "joke," only to immediately apologize and comfort you as soon as you react. They then bring you flowers as an "apology" and reassure you that they care for you. As soon as you forgive them, they start calling you even worse names again. Or they may subject you to a prolonged silent treatment, causing you to reach out to them out of anxiety and a fear of abandonment. They may ignore your phone calls, heightening your anxiety for a long period of time. When you finally withdraw from the relationship, they sense you're about to leave them, so they "comfort" you with more gifts, apologies, or "makeup sex" just to meet their own needs and keep you trapped in the cycle.

As the narcissist and you become *enmeshed*, they distort your sense of self and you forego parts of your identity. You sacrifice your authentic self to keep holding on to the relationship, often acting out of character in response to prolonged manipulation. For example, you may start to display behaviors that stem from your anger and resentment in the relationship. You may feel more easily triggered when the narcissist disappoints you (understandably so) because of the larger pattern of them provoking you. You might find yourself trying to micromanage or control them because of the jealousy induction you endured. For example, you might request they stop hanging out with the suspicious friends they tried to provoke you with or ask for their location. In a healthy relationship, you wouldn't even need to ask, as healthy partners wouldn't be surrounding themselves with shady exes or making you feel distrustful on a daily basis.

The boundaries you started out with when the relationship first began may have included standards like "I would never allow a partner to speak down to me," or "If a partner ever tries to make me jealous or betrays me, I'll leave," yet due to the intensity of the trauma bond, you find that you've abandoned these standards in order to maintain the relationship. The narcissist encourages this and becomes further enmeshed with you as they instill an "It's us against the world" mentality, isolating you from friends and family members who are rightfully concerned about your relationship. You subconsciously grow closer to them because you feel like others don't support you (in reality, they just don't believe the relationship is healthy for you), and your abuser trains you to view others as "the enemy." This is like the reversal of the love bombing stage; whereas before the narcissist mirrored *you*, now you are forced to become more like *them* or who *they* want you to be in order to survive the trauma of the relationship.

Dangerous Adaptation and Learned Helplessness

In this stage, your continual sacrifices and PTSD symptoms keep you *dangerously adapted* to the relationship, protecting or defending the abuser, rationalizing their behavior, and returning to them over and over. This is usually the final stage of trauma bonding before steps are made toward healing. By this stage, you have made immense sacrifices of your time, energy, labor, and resources, and that can be hard to walk away from. You've likely spent months or even years planning a future with this person, encouraging and helping them, all while abandoning your own self-care. This investment can be difficult for anyone in a trauma bond, but having children or shared finances with the narcissist presents additional obstacles.

The sunk-cost fallacy, as described above, leads you to believe that all the harm and trauma in the relationship represents the fact that this is a relationship worth continuing because subconsciously you feel the need to justify your investment. You begin to heavily sabotage yourself and self-destruct because you start to believe in the lies the narcissist has fed you about your worthiness and lovability. You may even defend or protect the abuser to loved ones who express concern for your well-being. You might fear retaliation because of threats the narcissist has made or any information the narcissist could use against you. You may return to the narcissist several times before you leave for good.

Because trauma has also burdened you with symptoms like fatigue, brain fog, hypervigilance, irritability, anxiety, depression, and constant exhaustion, it feels easier to stay in the relationship to try to make it work rather than taking the seemingly impossible steps to leave. You have learned that whatever you do to improve or leave the relationship backfires, and you become stuck in *learned hopelessness*. Therefore, your patterns of behaving and existing now revolve around the narcissist and how to cope with the relationship rather than breaking ties.

The Connection Between Intimate Partner Violence and Torture Tactics

Narcissists intensify the trauma bond through monopolizing your attention and internal resources by manufacturing chaos. Like a cat that plays with a mouse, narcissists and psychopaths enjoy provoking chaos and feeding off the emotional fuel they get from instigating emotional reactions in people. When you're too exhausted from navigating their mind games and diversion tactics, you're much less likely to take care of yourself or tend to your needs.

They can manufacture chaos in multiple ways, such as the following:

- They create irrelevant, crazy-making arguments out of thin air that seem to go on for hours.

- This can include false accusations and intensive interrogation, or attempts to provoke you with inappropriate comments or jokes followed by gaslighting of your reactions as "crazy" or "oversensitive."

- They deprive you of sleep, especially before important events.

These destabilizing manipulation methods overlap with the ones weaponized against prisoners of war, according to sociologist and researcher Albert D. Biderman. Biderman developed a Chart of Coercion that shows the similarities between what domestic violence victims go through (albeit on a much smaller scale) and the tactics used on prisoners of war (Baldwin et al. 2015). Although the experiences of prisoners of war cannot be equated to domestic violence survivors, due to the severity and harm involved and the fact that such tactics tend to be far more extreme, there are crucial parallels to consider that help us better understand the overwhelming and debilitating nature of these tactics.

Manipulation Tactics According to the Chart of Coercion

Let's compare how each of the following coercive methods from Biderman's research corresponds to the manipulation tactics narcissists and psychopaths specifically use, albeit on a much smaller scale.

Isolation. Prisoners of war endure solitary confinement or isolation with a group to deprive them of social support. Similarly, on a much less extreme level, domestic abuse survivors can also be isolated by their abusers through verbal and emotional abuse as well as physical threats to keep them reliant on the abuser. In extreme cases, some survivors are kept physically isolated from the outside world to prevent them from making social connections or gaining employment.

Monopolization of perception. Prisoners are restricted in their movements, the food they eat, and the light and environment they're exposed to. This compels them to focus their attention on their current state and silences resistance over time. It also keeps them ignorant of information that might make them noncompliant with demands. Although domestic violence survivors are not necessarily physically restricted, they can be emotionally manipulated and coerced into only focusing on the abuser and shielded from information, support networks, and resources that could help them.

Humiliation and degradation. Demeaning punishment and taunting in response to self-protection or self-defense make resistance to abuse and authority more costly than obedience. Victims of abuse find themselves so diminished by the onslaught of emotional torment that they start to shrink themselves and internalize the abuser's perception of them.

Exhaustion. Starving prisoners and depriving them of sleep or sub-jecting them to lengthy interrogations overexerts their resources so they are unable to resist. As you'll learn, narcissists use similar but less extreme tools in romantic relationships to keep their victims too exhausted and debilitated to fight back or engage in the self-care needed to defend themselves in healthy ways.

Threats. Prisoners of war are threatened with physical violence—both against themselves and their families—as well as abandonment. The threats of physical violence, as well as emotional abuse and abandonment, play a key role in sustaining trauma bonds with narcissists. Since narcissists tap into our deepest abandonment wounds and cause anxiety about our survival and any resources we have been taught to rely on them for, we walk on eggshells around them to prevent harm.

Occasional indulgences. Prisoners are given occasional "rewards" or favors, as well as false promises, when they are especially compliant. This keeps their hope alive but also reinforces obedient behavior. As we talked about earlier, intermittent reinforcement keeps victims biochemically and psychologically hooked to their abusers.

Demonstrating omnipotence. Control is exerted over prisoners through dominance. Prisoners learn that resistance is essentially futile. Similarly, narcissists and psychopaths also display dominance through manipulation tactics such as silent treatments, rage attacks, and retaliation when their victims do not cater to their sense of entitlement. This teaches their victims that resisting will only lead to further retaliation and punishment; speaking up or setting boundaries always comes with a price.

Forcing trivial demands. Even the smallest rules must be obeyed, or punishment will ensue. The punishment for prisoners of war is far more dire and lethal, but survivors of abusive relationships can definitely relate to this on a much smaller scale. The narcissist or psychopath compels their victims to do the same, making mountains out of molehills and hypercriticizing their victims over irrelevant and miniscule matters to condition them into perpetual compliance.

How Narcissists and Psychopaths Use Manipulation Tactics

Let's look at the most common manipulation methods narcissists and psychopaths use, and how they parallel the tactics used on prisoners of war that we just discussed.

Humiliation, Degradation, and Exhaustion

Some of the ways narcissists and psychopaths use the torture tactics of humiliation, degradation, and exhaustion are through crazy-making arguments, inducing jealousy, and violating your boundaries to keep you off-kilter and too exhausted to fight back. Here are some examples of how these methods can be used.

Crazy-making arguments. The narcissist wants you to exhaust yourself and overexplain yourself during crazy-making arguments they manufacture out of seemingly nowhere. That is why they will purposely bait you with contradictory or triggering information and then proceed to talk in circles and gaslight you, depicting you as crazy. You begin to question what they mean and ask for clarification, but the fact is there is no clarity in this orchestrated confusion. No matter how politely or calmly you respond or inquire about the motives and meaning behind these claims, they'll frame your curiosity as an "interrogation." They will display the "cold" rage psychopathy experts note is shallow. What does this do? This conditions you to stop asking questions altogether and walk on eggshells around them. It ensures that your voice is silenced, your needs and wants are not considered, and you are less likely to come forward with your concerns in the future. It keeps you in your "place."

Yet you may notice that even when you do not react to the narcissist's provocations, they poke and prod further or seem disappointed. That's because, in reality, they actually *want* you to ask more about this unsettling information. They want you to react so they can gain a sense of power and control.

Christopher is a narcissistic lawyer who likes to make his longtime girlfriend, Natalie, feel jealous and off-kilter. He has always felt like Natalie was out of his league and wants to make sure he always has the upper hand in the relationship. One day, he stages a conversation with Natalie about a new female coworker who has just started working at his firm. He drops hints to Natalie that he plans to have lunch with this coworker. Natalie asks him casually what the lunch will be about, and Christopher immediately flies into a rage, telling Natalie that she is "interrogating" him and calling her "insecure," "crazy," and "jealous." He stonewalls her, saying, "I can't do this with you anymore. You're being too controlling and paranoid," and storms out of the house. Natalie is perplexed as she was just trying to show interest in his work life and was being calm and polite while doing so. To an outsider, this scene looks bizarre, and it is. That's because Christopher set it up to get a reaction from Natalie, no matter how minor and calm, and depict that reaction in a way that serves his gaslighting purposes.

Christopher set up bait for Natalie to respond to and when she did react, even in a gentle and curious manner, he punishes her for doing exactly what he wants her to do. Christopher isn't actually angry at Natalie's questions; he's putting on a manufactured display of cold rage to make her feel paranoid, insecure, and jealous, even if she displays confidence. He knows how to frame her simple questions as an "interrogation." This kills two birds with one stone: it conditions Natalie to walk on eggshells, making her reluctant to ask basic questions or express her emotions in the relationship, and it gives Christopher power and control. He has essentially gained leverage to engage in shady behavior in the future by instilling fear in Natalie about holding him accountable. She now knows the "consequences" of confronting him about his behavior and knows there will be retaliation.

Inducing jealousy. Narcissists and psychopaths are adept at deceiving their loved ones. Many lead double lives that may remain hidden for months, years, or even decades. They blame you for questioning them or setting boundaries in response to their shady behavior. Jealousy induction makes you compete for the narcissist and seek their validation instead of spending your energy detaching from the relationship and getting out. It's a powerful tool that entraps and trauma bonds you to the narcissist, as it makes you see the narcissist as "valuable" even if you were previously not as interested in them. That's because the narcissist or psychopath forces you to compare yourself to others and has created an aura of desirability by mentioning previous and current members of their harem.

Your ability to identify their red flags and mistreatment of you becomes diminished as you become conditioned to see the narcissist or psychopath as the "valuable" one—someone you have to "win" over regardless of their heinous transgressions—even if you have more options than they do and surpass them in many aspects. This makes you more trauma bonded to them, as you fear the loss of their attention more than the loss of your own identity and self-confidence.

Violating boundaries. Healthy relationships require boundaries that make people feel safe on *both* sides. In a relationship with a narcissist, the concept of "boundaries" gets weaponized to force you to distrust your instincts. For example, if you notice that your narcissistic partner is taking late-night calls, you may question who they are talking to, especially if they have a habit of being deceptive or telling white lies. Due to your valid suspicions and distrust, you might ask your partner to show you their phone or at least offer an explanation. However, the narcissist is likely to respond with rage and call you paranoid and controlling.

While it's true that some behaviors can be controlling in relationships, calling out behavior that violates your boundaries, putting your emotional and physical safety and health at risk, is not one of them. If someone has given you plenty of reasons to distrust them and this is part of a larger pattern, you have a right to ensure that they're not deceiving you. You have every right to ask questions or request more information. It's not invasive or "controlling" to set boundaries or hold someone accountable for deceptive behavior while in a committed relationship.

Isolation

Narcissists and psychopaths use the torture tactic of isolation to gain the upper hand in the relationship. They'll use destructive conditioning to deflate your feelings of joy and accomplishment and make you dependent on them for your sense of self. They'll also alienate you from loved ones and make you feel like you're the only one who has a problem with them.

Sabotaging you and making you dependent. Narcissists and psychopaths attempt to spoil your joy during holidays, special occasions, and celebrations so you're unable to seek fulfillment outside of them. They love toying with and provoking their victims during these memorable moments so that they remain the center of attention. That's why they'll suddenly begin rageful arguments leading up to Thanksgiving and become a depressed Grinch during Christmas, spreading negativity and spite to their loved ones. It's also why they'll diminish one of your big accomplishments or even compare you to someone else to ensure you associate your accomplishment with this degrading comparison rather than enjoying the fruits of your labor. Whether it's hurling crazy-making accusations before a holiday party to disorient you, comparing you to others to diminish your sense of achievement, or deliberately withholding affection and attention when you get a job promotion, these pathological personalities know exactly how to deflate your joy so the focus is on them once more.

Destructive conditioning. Narcissistic and psychopathic individuals punish you for experiencing joy outside of them. That is why they attempt to pair your joyful moments with terror, abuse, criticism, and minimizing remarks. They want to destructively condition you to associate the experience of gaining validation and pleasure from sources outside of them with experiencing fear, distress, and their rage. This is also due to their pathological envy and the sadistic pleasure they derive from attempting to deflate your excitement. That is why narcissistic and psychopathic individuals are notorious for ruining holidays, special celebrations, and birthdays. Remember, toxic people always feel a compulsive need to destroy beautiful moments to better isolate you, control you, get you to associate joy with their punishment, and make you dependent on only them for fulfillment.

Alienating you from loved ones. A key component of the trauma bond is isolation. Narcissists can isolate you physically from the outside world but they also isolate you figuratively. They strip you of your identity, degrade the healthy and positive feedback you receive from others, and ensure that you no longer feel comfortable around those who love and support you. They might claim your friends and family are just "jealous" of your relationship and are trying to tear you apart. They may make false accusations, implying that nobody in your inner circle actually likes or supports you, even though this is far from the truth. They may stage false comparisons while declaring that "no one else has ever had a problem like this with them." This is a way to make sure you don't leave them. When you begin to feel like the problem, you stop seeing the true problem (*them*) accurately. You feel defective, different, and separate from those around you.

By gaslighting you using this tactic, they're able to paradoxically pull you closer to them. You feel subconsciously conditioned to seek their reassurance after this claim and further entrenched in the relationship and tethered to them. You may be misled into believing that your reactions to the abuse are the problem, and become further bonded to them as you increase your efforts to prove to them that you are *not* the problem. In reality, you do have people who support and love you, and people who have been terrorized by the narcissist have usually experienced the same vindictive and aggressive behaviors you have. Should you ever talk to any of their other victims about their experiences, you'll soon find out these stories showcase eerily similar behavioral patterns indicating their lack of empathy, callousness, cruelty, and degradation of others.

Monopolization of Perception and Omnipotence

Narcissists and psychopaths monopolize your perceptions and make themselves seem omnipotent by eroding your identity, distorting your sense of self, and corroding your self-esteem.

Eroding and distorting your identity. Narcissistic and psychopathic individuals do not always abuse in a way that is outwardly obvious. That is why they engage in underhanded methods to take control over your mind and erode your sense of self and identity over time. This is a key component of the trauma bond, as researchers note that trauma-bonded victims adopt the perspectives of their perpetrators rather than staying grounded in their own sense of self.

One of these tactics is the method of *distortion*, a way of making you see yourself as the opposite of what you actually are, in·an attempt to lower your self-esteem so that you are more compliant and malleable to their demands. Narcissists will distort your true traits and behaviors to depict you as the opposite of who you are. Ironically, their accusations tend to be a projection of their own behaviors, traits, and character. You may notice that their accusations contradict the feedback you get from empathic people who have no agenda to gaslight or control you. While others may comment on your kindness, empathy, integrity, intelligence, and generosity, the narcissist may claim you are selfish (especially when you start setting healthy boundaries with them), deceptive, or lacking in some way—all claims that better describe them.

This is a way to isolate you from the healthy and accurate feedback and support they know you have so they can control your self-perception—and better control you. Imagine the narcissistic individual metaphorically placing a funhouse mirror in front of you to "distort" your true proportions. This is exactly what they are doing when they engage in covert insults or make comparisons to you and something else that represents the opposing qualities of what you actually are. For example, a covert narcissist may do this by commenting on a positive trait you possess by implying you're the opposite (e.g., "You're no fun," or "You're not very social" when you are in fact outgoing and popular). Or they may compare you physically or emotionally to someone you could not be more different from to underhandedly diminish you.

Distortion can happen in a number of ways, but the motive is the same: to destabilize you and plant self-doubt, especially about positive qualities you possess and the positive qualities *others* notice about you and celebrate. This is a way to alienate you even when you are surrounded by support and healthy praise from others. By alienating you, you become further trauma bonded to the narcissist for comfort and approval as they become your primary source of validation and feedback for your sense of self.

Corroding your self-esteem. Narcissists and psychopaths affect your sense of self. It's likely that before this relationship, you felt much more confident and self-assured. Your emotions were balanced and stable. During the abuse cycle, you've become more reactive and uncertain, doubtful of your self-worth and battling insecurities you previously would have never considered. Now, you find yourself constantly comparing yourself to others due to your partner's cruel and callous comments. You scrutinize yourself frequently, seeing yourself through their distorted lens. You become conditioned over time to think about what the narcissist or psychopath thinks, wants, and feels—and forget about your own desires, emotions, values, and boundaries. This is because they've gaslit you into believing you are crazy for having desires, emotions, values, and boundaries in the first place. By deflating your confidence, narcissists and psychopaths are able to diminish partners who are out of their league in many ways into staying in the abusive relationship.

Threats and Self-Harm

Psychopaths specifically are likely to push you into self-harm, reckless activity, or substance use. As mentioned previously, these types require extra stimulation and are prone to boredom. Not only do they pursue high-risk activities themselves to obtain that stimulation, but they also want to encourage it in others for their sadistic pleasure. They want to see how far they can push you toward harm, especially when you are most vulnerable. They do this for their entertainment, playing the puppeteer to your emotions, actions, and reactions.

This coercion can happen in a number of different ways. They encourage you to self-sabotage during important goals (e.g., they may encourage you to party before big exams or interviews). They may subtly push you toward self-harm for their own pleasure or show callous indifference during crises when you are already feeling over the edge. In extreme cases, they may push you to self-mutilate or, even more sadistically, encourage suicide. They may "innocently" suggest or persuade you into reckless behavior that could harm yourself or others, like drunk driving or vandalism, or excessive substance use. At times, they will engage in these activities themselves and frame you for doing them, or coerce you into them only to try to blackmail you or threaten you with exposure. For example, some survivors have noted that their abusers threatened to tell their employers that they were drug addicts (even in cases that was not true) to have more control over them.

Narcissistic and psychopathic individuals may also blame their abuse of you on external factors, such as stress or being under the influence of substances. However, you must understand that they are able to control their behavior with those they need to maintain their image around, such as employers or friends they want to impress. That means their use of substances is usually weaponized to disguise their abuse. It's their core lack of empathy and remorse, not substance use, that is the root of the problem here.

Research reveals that unlike those who are nonpsychopathic, psychopathic individuals may not develop the same types of drug cravings or withdrawal symptoms as most people suffering from addiction do, and their brains are activated differently in response to drug-related cues (Cope et al. 2014; Vincent et al. 2018). Psychopaths also turn to substances because they have a greater need for sensation-seeking behaviors and are prone to boredom, while narcissists may use substances to seek an emotional high. Both types may use substances as a justification to instigate violence.

Narcissists and psychopaths use substance abuse coercion to not only keep you under the influence, but to also keep you under *their* influence and detract from your credibility. When you are under the influence of drugs and alcohol, you experience less inhibition and more memory impairment, which makes you compliant to more of their abuse, whether it's verbal, psychological, physical, or sexual. This is an insidious control method that allows them to isolate and gaslight you more readily because you cannot trust your memory or perception of the abuse. They can encourage substance use to restrict your ability to gain employment, micromanage your finances, threaten your custody of children, or portray you as the abuser to law enforcement.

Abandonment during vulnerable moments. Many stories abound of narcissistic and psychopathic individuals abandoning their loved ones in times of great need, such as during a health crisis, in the beginning of a pregnancy, during a loss or a miscarriage, or in the middle of nowhere on vacation. They may also threaten to abandon you in these circumstances to keep you compliant and silent about their mistreatment and negligence. They may even abandon you when you are about to celebrate a life-changing achievement or milestone (such as an important anniversary or a graduation). This level of callousness and inhumanity traumatizes many survivors. Some narcissists and psychopaths take a special glee in abandoning you when you most need them, as these are times when they feel they are no longer the center of attention or can no longer milk you for resources and labor.

Dog Whistling

In politics, the term *dog whistle* refers to coded language. A dog whistle is a subtle signal to communicate something that is seemingly innocent but has a message that is too controversial to be laid out transparently, much like how a literal dog whistle is a high-pitched whistle with a frequency that makes it audible to dogs but not humans. In the context of abusive relationships with narcissists, dog whistles are often used in public, in front of groups, online, or even one-on-one to mock and degrade you underhandedly. By using dog whistling, they are able to keep you under their control while escaping accountability for their actions. Here are some examples of dog whistling you may have experienced in a relationship with a narcissist or psychopath.

Insulting you in front of others. Narcissists and psychopaths gain a special kind of duping delight from being able to put you down in public without facing any consequences or harm to their reputation. If you try to confront them, they will depict you as unhinged, especially if the people around you don't understand what they are referencing. For example, a woman who is emotionally abused by her husband may encounter a dog whistle from him when they go to a dinner party. Behind closed doors, he regularly makes insulting remarks about her weight gain and criticizes her body. In front of others, he might make a seemingly "playful" remark about how many appetizers she's been eating. Their mutual friends might laugh, thinking it's just a joke. However, the wife understands the underlying meaning in this so-called "joke" and feels deflated, feeling the full force of all the criticism both behind closed doors and in public. Should she dare call out her husband, he will likely feign innocence and establish plausible deniability, pretending that she misinterpreted his intentions.

Instilling a sense of fear. Narcissists like to keep their partners off-balance, and one way they do this is by making them fear their wrath. For example, a narcissistic mother might give her son a certain "look" when he is playing too loudly in front of other relatives, indicating that she will physically punish him later on, as this is the same look she gives him right before she physically strikes him behind closed doors. A narcissistic professor who is sexually abusing one of his students might speak loudly about how certain papers were better than others, winking at the student he is grooming to let her know that she will have to do special favors to "earn" her grade. These are all subtle ways to establish dominance over the victim.

Retraumatizing your wounds. Narcissists and psychopaths are masters of rubbing salt on your wounds: they provoke you on purpose to taunt you and feel a sense of power at observing your reactions to them. If the manipulator in your life is well aware of your triggers, they will use them against you. There isn't a limit to how far they will go. For example, if you've been sexually assaulted or violated, they may start dishing out victim-blaming remarks or begin coercing you into sexual activities you're not comfortable with. If you've disclosed an insecurity (such as about a facial feature or body part), they could start making cruel jokes about that perceived flaw, only to call you "too sensitive" when you protest. These inhumane digs would be off-limits to most empathic human beings, but not to them. These are all calculated moves to retraumatize you.

Comparing you to others in demeaning ways. We know that narcissists want you to compete for them. That's why they'll also use dog whistling to reference an external or internal quality or ability that their exes or present prospects have so they can highlight a perceived shortcoming or flaw in you. This doesn't mean you actually have any kind of shortcoming or that their critical comments are valid; it just means that the narcissist wants you to compare yourself to others and compete for their attention and approval. They might mention how their ex-spouse always cooked and cleaned up after them to get you to take on more domestic duties. They might call your attention to someone in public who looks different from you, making you feel like you aren't enough. Or whenever you mention an accomplishment, they might subtly change the subject to someone else's achievement entirely to deflate your joy. In reality, they are likely to pull this antic when they know *they* aren't enough for you or they perceive you to be out of their league.

Provoking you through social media. Social media isn't just social media. It's a highly public platform that can be used for the greater good or can amplify toxicity. It's also the perfect playground for narcissists and psychopaths to use dog whistling. They will abuse the "like," "follow," "comment," and "direct message" functions to induce jealousy in you, following inappropriate accounts or sliding into the direct messages of other people. They will also send you memes, pictures, and videos designed to poke at your insecurities. For example, a narcissistic man might send his female partner photos or videos of scantily clad women under the guise of a "joke." Or a narcissistic woman might comment frequently under pictures of their ex-boyfriend while ignoring your messages. Narcissistic partners may also publish posts or stories that reference your relationship in covert and demeaning ways, falsely mischaracterizing you to others.

These dog whistles help establish power over you and humiliate you in front of others, making you feel even more isolated in the relationship. Should you express outrage, the narcissist or psychopath can easily gaslight you into believing you're overreacting, and can paint you as neurotic and "obsessed" to others. In reality, this behavior is disrespectful, whether it takes place online or in real life.

How Narcissists Use Manipulation Tactics to Strengthen Trauma Bonds

The reason narcissists know exactly which trigger buttons to push is because they installed them in the first place. Unbeknownst to you, they have identified which trigger phrases, events, and insecurities to mention in order to provoke and unsettle you, depicting you as "crazy" or "unhinged" when you finally do react. During the abuse cycle, they implant insecurities in you and watch you unravel as you fixate on them. They do this so chronically that you are constantly scrambling to defend, react, and overexplain yourself, becoming too exhausted to detach from the relationship.

By manufacturing chaos through provoking you, they gain leverage. As you spend most of your time and energy navigating their diversion tactics, defending yourself against their claims, and trying to skirt their sabotage, they take up your mental resources, so you are only focused on them and the relationship and have less time for yourself, your goals, your healing, and your self-care. You have less time to recover from the abuse when it's ongoing, frequent, or impactful, so you become too exhausted to fight back as effectively. Your only option seems to be going to the source of pain itself (the abuser) in an attempt to survive the abuse.

You also seek comfort from your abuser due to their hurt-and-rescue methods. They deliberately wound you, then come to the rescue with their comfort, fake apologies, and promises to never do it again, only to start the cycle once more. This uncertainty keeps you perpetually off-kilter and dependent on their validation, negotiating your self-respect and basic needs with the abuser to avoid being swallowed whole.

All of these tactics are part of the powerful trauma bond you develop with your abuser as a survival mechanism. The trauma bond becomes even stronger as you subconsciously justify your investment in them as a relationship "worth" fighting for despite all the obstacles they subject you to.

How to Weaken the Trauma Bond

Use the acronym SAFE to remember to behave in ways that weaken rather than strengthen the trauma bond and allow you to react more mindfully.

Sensitize yourself to cruelty.

Appraise rather than appease.

Flee and fade out when possible.

Energize and enrich yourself.

S: Sensitize

Sensitizing yourself to the narcissist's cruelty is all about slowly re-sensitizing yourself to the horror and outrage you would have experienced prior to the trauma bond. It's likely there are a number of mechanisms, including some level of dissociation and suppression, that are taking place to protect you from the true pain and anger you would otherwise experience in response to the narcissist's actions. Through their manipulation tactics, the narcissist has created a situation in which your boundaries have been eroded to the point where transgressions that were previously unacceptable have become the "new normal." This new normal has likely been sustained by a number of subconscious rationalizations, justifications, and minimizations to maintain the relationship and your own sense of coping and survival. Re-sensitizing yourself is about gradually grounding yourself in the reality of the relationship, recalling the boundary violations that have occurred, and working to see betrayal as an unacceptable part of your self-concept and relationships. Part of this may involve working with a mental health professional and using some of the healing modalities outlined in chapter 4.

A: Appraise Rather Than Appease

Appraising reminds you that you have options other than *appeasing* the narcissist. While there are times that the fawn survival response will help you navigate these toxic types and their manipulation tactics, it's important to take a more detached, critical perspective when appraising the pros and cons of engaging in any interaction or behavior with the narcissist. This means habitually *increasing the gap between their actions and your responses* whenever possible to mindfully become aware of your triggers and emotions, and choosing an action that benefits you or your loved ones in your specific circumstances. This will recondition you to step outside of constant fight, flight, freeze, or fawn mode and provide some space to respond without the narcissist's interference. Remember: the narcissist's goal is to evoke a response—whether negative or positive. Your goal is to minimize their significance and impact on your life as much as possible.

F: Flee and Fade Out

Flee is a reminder to avoid contact with the narcissist as much as possible. No matter what your circumstances may be or how long you've been in the relationship, the ultimate goal is harm reduction and prevention as you weaken the trauma bond. It's essential that you reduce the significance of the narcissist's impact on your life, your energy, and your time, even if you are in a situation where you are co-parenting or working with the narcissist. You can set a limit for how much time you spend every day on the narcissist (whether by interacting with them, engaging in compulsive actions that react to their behavior, or ruminating over them). Decrease this limit over time if this task seems too overwhelming at first (e.g., start with limiting your interactions and engagement with the narcissist to only thirty minutes, and gradually reduce it to twenty, ten, and so forth).

If you're forced to make contact, *fade out* reminds you that you have a choice in responding with brief, factual responses that don't engage the narcissist's need for negative attention or drain your energy. Creating this distance is pertinent to reconnecting with your own sense of identity, which has been eroded throughout the relationship, in a graduated manner that does not overwhelm your nervous system.

E: Energize and Enrich Yourself

Use the empowering self-care and healing modalities discussed in the next chapter to recenter and ground yourself. Use these activities daily to "level up" your physical and mental health and create a rewarding life for yourself outside of the narcissist. This will give you more incentive to weaken the trauma bond as toxic interactions with the narcissist detract from energizing and enriching yourself.

Takeaways

If you are in a trauma bond with a narcissist or psychopath, you are not alone and support is out there. You must connect to your authentic outrage at being violated and get in touch with the reality of the abuse in order to begin breaking a trauma bond, but the first step is to recognize that such a bond exists in the first place. That's what this chapter aimed to do, describing the neuroscience and stages of trauma bonding, the connection between intimate partner violence and torture tactics, and how narcissists and psychopaths use these tactics to manipulate their partners and strengthen trauma bonds even more.

In the next chapter, you'll learn specific evidence-based tools to navigate these manipulation tactics, take your power back, and heal from a trauma bond.

CHAPTER 4

Healing from the Trauma Bond

You've learned a lot about the intricacies of abusive relationships with narcissists and psychopaths and the powerful trauma bonds we develop to them. But how do you heal? It's important that you not only understand the tactics of the manipulation you endured, but also how to handle these tactics and heal. Healing may seem impossible because you've been in survival mode for so long. But I want you to know it's more than possible and the pain that you are experiencing now doesn't have to be the pain you experience forever. Many survivors do heal from these relationships and go on to live even more thriving and successful lives. They jump-start their careers, improve their mental health, find healthy relationships, and even give back to the greater good and spread awareness of what they've learned. They work on their self-esteem, health, fitness, personal and professional goals, and skyrocket their self-care. Some even manifest the life of their dreams. They not only heal, they *level up*.

In this chapter, we'll first discuss the diverse healing modalities you can use to help break the trauma bond, followed by an overview of nine major steps survivors usually take on their journey to break the trauma bond. You will find numerous exercises that will help you implement these steps in practical, research-backed ways.

Traditional Healing Modalities for Trauma Bonding

Below you will find evidence-based healing modalities that can help you heal from the effects of trauma in a relationship with a narcissist or psychopath. What works best for one survivor may not be the same as for another survivor. When in doubt, consult with a trauma-informed professional to determine which modality is best for you and your circumstances.

Eye Movement Desensitization and Reprocessing Therapy (EMDR)

Eye movement desensitization and reprocessing therapy (EMDR) is a specialized trauma-processing therapy. It was first developed around 1990 by Francine Shapiro, who noticed side-to-side eye movements had the effect of decreasing the impact of recalling disturbing traumatic memories in the present moment and also reduced their impact over time. As you learned in chapter 1, traumatic memories can be maladaptively stored in the brain. According to Shapiro's adaptive information processing model, these traumatic memories are not processed rationally in the prefrontal cortex as other memories are (Hill 2020). EMDR helps integrate and process memories, thoughts, emotions, and sensations related to the traumatic event that may feel disconnected and fragmented so your triggers are no longer as overwhelming.

In EMDR, clients are asked to remember traumatic or distressing events while making side-to-side eye movements or using left-to-right hand tapping; these bilateral movements are said to help your brain bypass the heightened emotionality of the amygdala. Using a complex eight-step process, EMDR allows you to access the traumatic memory network and integrate your trauma without being as overwhelmed by your emotional reactions to it. This reduces emotional distress while healthier associations with traumatic memories are formed. EMDR targets present, past, and future, since clients are asked to address past events that have caused distress in addition to present triggers and evaluate the beliefs that stemmed from these traumatic events, then they are asked to incorporate new beliefs to better serve them going forward. This may help you process key traumas that may be affecting your behavior and strengthening the trauma bond so you feel unable to leave the toxic relationship.

EMDR has been shown by randomized clinical trials to be potentially effective for reducing PTSD symptoms (Hill 2020). Speak to a therapist about EMDR and how it can help you reach a state of emotional balance.

Cognitive Behavioral Therapy (CBT), Cognitive Processing Therapy (CPT), and Prolonged Exposure Therapy (PET)

Developed by Aaron Beck in the 1960s, cognitive behavioral therapy (CBT) helps us identify and target maladaptive emotions, behaviors, and thoughts, reforming them to better suit our boundaries and self-esteem (Beck & Fleming 2021). Studies indicate that CBT is effective for depression, anxiety, eating disorders, and relationship issues, all of which can be potential concerns for survivors of narcissists (Nakao, Shirotsuki, & Sugaya 2021). Strategies of CBT can include reforming cognitive distortions, role-playing, exposure to fears, and learning to calm the body during stressful events (Clark & Beck 2010).

While CBT in the form of talk therapy alone may not always be the most effective for survivors of narcissistic abuse (who usually need more specialized treatment from a professional who deeply understands narcissistic abuse), CBT can help address cognitive distortions created by gaslighting and manipulation, provided that the therapist you're working with is trauma-informed and well-versed in the dynamics of abuse and manipulation.

Another evidence-based therapy that may be effective for abuse survivors is cognitive processing therapy (CPT), which is helpful for those who have PTSD symptoms. CPT helps clients identify and work through maladaptive beliefs about trauma and avoidance behaviors.

Prolonged exposure therapy (PET), another evidence-based therapy, helps clients with PTSD become gradually desensitized to trauma-related memories, feelings, and situations. This gradual exposure allows them to prevent the avoidant behaviors that can otherwise sustain PTSD symptoms. Both CPT and PET have been shown by meta-analyses to substantially improve PTSD symptoms (McLean et al. 2022; Asmundson et al. 2019).

Dialectical Behavior Therapy (DBT)

Dialectical behavior therapy (DBT) is an evidence-based form of cognitive behavioral therapy developed by therapist Marsha Linehan. It was designed to target vulnerable populations who struggle with intense, overwhelming emotions, self-harm, and suicidal ideation. DBT merges Eastern mindfulness techniques with cognitive behavioral methods and focuses on four modules: (1) mindfulness, (2) distress tolerance, (3) emotion regulation, and (4) interpersonal effectiveness (McKay, Wood, & Brantley 2021).

Using a combination of individual therapy sessions, group therapy, and intensive homework exercises, DBT provides the crucial tools for enhancing your emotion regulation and reducing your emotional vulnerability so you have a better sense of control in your daily life as you heal. Although it's widely used with patients who have borderline personality disorder, DBT's skills can be used by anyone and everyone, including abuse survivors. Randomized clinical trials indicate that DBT is life-saving for those struggling with self-harm, suicidal ideation, and post-traumatic stress disorder symptoms (May, Richardi, & Barth 2016). You may find DBT especially helpful if you're having trouble with emotion regulation or struggling with self-harm due to the abuse you suffered.

This form of therapy helps you regulate and cope with your emotions, improve your interpersonal effectiveness skills, and stay grounded in the present moment during crises. DBT group therapy sessions allow you to practice and role-play the skills you've learned, providing coping and communication strategies for interactions with difficult people you can't avoid.

EXERCISE: Learn DBT Skills

Many of the skills taught in dialectical behavior therapy (DBT) can be very helpful when you are trying to break the trauma bond and regulate your emotions. You can also download this exercise at http://www.newharbin ger.com/53561.

- **Temperature control.** Hold an ice cube in your hand, immerse your face in cold water, or take a cold shower to jolt your mind back to the present moment.

- **Mindfulness.** Take a nonjudgmental "observer" stance to what is happening around you. To begin, first name the emotion you're experiencing. Notice the colors, sounds, and scents around you. Envision your thoughts are just words on a cloud floating past you.

- **Muscle relaxation.** Tense up your muscles in an exaggerated way and then let them go. This helps you pinpoint where the most tension lies so you can start releasing and relaxing those parts of your body.

- **Emotion regulation.** List your various options for how you can respond during conflict or a distressing experience. This is more of a rhetorical exercise to remind you that you always have some choices available to you. You can change the situation or work to change your emotions. No matter how distressing a situation may be, you do have options on how to respond—including doing nothing. Ironically, this sense of freedom often gives you the motivation to take effective action and own your full power and agency in the situation.

- **Reduce emotional vulnerability.** Locate opportunities to increase positive emotions, engage in self-soothing methods, identify dysregulated emotions, and overcome your fears. These activities will strengthen you and your resolve to detach from the trauma bond.

- **Create a sleep schedule.** Good sleep is vital for your brain, mood, memory, and overall health. When your sleep is disrupted, you tend to respond to even low-stress situations in ways individuals who do have a healthy sleep routine respond to high-stress ones. People with PTSD often struggle with sleep problems—whether it's sleeping too much or not sleeping enough. Narcissists may also deliberately interfere with your sleep by starting arguments or tampering with your ability to sleep. You can enhance your sleep by sticking to a schedule, engaging in soothing rituals before bedtime, avoiding electronics and caffeine before bed, enhancing your sleep environment with white noise or soft lights, or speaking to your doctor about an appropriate sleep medication.

- **Journal.** Get out of your "emotion" brain and into your thinking one. Write down your thoughts when you feel conflicted, gaslit, and confused. Speak aloud to yourself as you work through a problem or situation, "advising" and encouraging yourself. This will tap into your prefrontal cortex and make it less likely for you to be hijacked by the emotion-driven parts of your brain.

Meditation

Research by Harvard neuroscientist Hölzel and colleagues (2011) revealed that a regular meditation practice such as a forty-minute daily meditation for eight weeks can decrease gray matter density in the amygdala, the part of our brain that manages our fight-or-flight response, and this is correlated with reductions in stress. It may also increase gray matter density in the hippocampus, helping with emotion regulation and memory formation, and increases gray matter in the frontal lobe, which could strengthen learning, planning, and focus (Hölzel et al. 2011; Tang, Friston, & Tang 2020). These changes in gray matter may lead to enhanced cognitive function and improved emotional regulation. According to a recent review, mindfulness-based treatments also strengthen connections between the default mode network (which plays a role in rumination) and the central executive and salience networks in individuals with PTSD (Boyd, Lanius, & McKinnon 2018). This strengthened connectivity helps individuals prepare effective responses to the threats of the outside world and is involved in enhancing emotional control, problem-solving, decision-making, and memory. The best part of meditation is that it's accessible to everyone: you can use guided meditation audios online or attend a meditation class.

However, some trauma survivors may not feel comfortable meditating if they are in a hypervigilant or avoidant state or struggle with intrusive thoughts. It's important to work with a therapist if that is the case to help process your trauma before beginning an active meditation practice. You may also benefit from starting with the following grounding exercises before you meditate to help train your brain to know that you are in a safe space when you do meditate.

GROUNDING EXERCISES

In these mindfulness exercises, you train your brain to remain in the present moment by grounding yourself in your surroundings. Here are three ways to ground yourself. This list and accompanying mindfulness meditations to counteract manipulation are also available at http://www.newharbinger.com/53561.

- Notice how each part of your body is supported by the chair, couch, or floor you're sitting or lying on. Notice how hard or soft this surface feels; observe the texture and the color.

- Look around you and notice one thing you see, hear, touch, taste, and smell.

- Scan your body and notice whether there is any tension in any places as you breathe normally. Exaggerate the tension, contracting your muscles, then let it go as you take a deep breath.

- If you want, you can continue to prolong your breath, visual-izing sending the energy of your breath as a healing force to places of tension in your body.

One of the most popular mindfulness interventions is the mindfulness-based stress reduction (MBSR) program, a supplementary treatment that combines meditation and yoga (see below) to create greater awareness of the present moment, enhance bodily awareness, reduce bodily tension, and regulate the stress response through breath and meditation.

MBSR has been shown to be effective for stress management, and researchers note that it targets two important pathways in the brain known as stress resilience pathways (Creswell et al. 2019). This includes the *regulatory pathway*, which regulates the fight-or-flight response through prefrontal cortex activity and connectivity, and the *reactivity pathway*, which includes areas of the brain where such stress responses originate. MBSR can enhance activation of the regulatory pathway while decreasing activity in the reactivity pathway, helping you control the stress response with better emotion regulation. Mindfulness interventions can change how your brain appraises stress, how you react to it physiologically, and how you cope.

Yoga

Yoga is an evidence-based and effective complementary treatment, especially for individuals with PTSD. A review of the research including a total of 4,434 participants demonstrated that yoga had a significant effect on decreasing PTSD symptoms (Laplaud et al. 2023). Studies show it can help reduce dissociation, aid in emotion regulation, improve sleep, and reduce tension throughout the body (Taylor et al. 2020; Kim et al. 2013; Rhodes, Spinazzola, & van der Kolk 2016; Zalta et al. 2018). It also gives you a sense of safety and mastery over your body, which allows you to mindfully approach your triggers. Whether you're doing yoga in the safety of your home using guided videos and audios or joining a yoga class with an instructor, gently ease into this practice with an open mind and observe whether it feels right for you and your needs.

Alternative Healing Modalities

The following therapies are considered more alternative treatments because they venture outside of the more mainstream and traditional therapeutic treatment models usually used to address trauma. However, many of these are still evidence-based and may be helpful for survivors.

Emotional Freedom Technique (EFT)

Created by Gary Craig, the emotional freedom technique helps you "tap" into various energy points in the body, releasing trapped energy and allowing electromagnetic energy to flow more readily throughout your body. Ultimately, this tapping method is said to clear harmful beliefs and replace them with healthier ones. If paired with positive affirmations (see below), EFT can help you reprogram what you believe you deserve and are worthy of in relationships, allowing you to set healthier boundaries with toxic partners. Emotional freedom technique has been shown across studies to improve physical health as well as emotional well-being (Bach et al. 2019).

Hypnotherapy

Hypnotherapy is a specialized therapy that incorporates guided hypnosis by a trained professional to place you in an altered state of consciousness or trance, which can help you calm your nervous system after trauma and also target deeply rooted subconscious beliefs and traumatic memories that may still be sabotaging you in the present moment. Hypnosis can supplement your healing journey in powerful ways, especially if you use it to rework destructive beliefs ingrained in you from the relationship with the narcissist as well as the fears you may have developed as a result of the toxic relationship.

Exercise

After trauma, your brain can suffer from neural atrophy, where the chronic elevation of stress hormones leads to impaired cognition and reduced neurogenesis, the birth of new neurons (Bremner 2006). This also leads to the decrease of brain-derived neurotrophic factor (BDNF), which, as you learned, is a key molecule that helps create changes in learning and memory through the rewiring of your brain and the birth of new neurons (Miranda et al. 2019). BDNF is like fertilizer for your brain, allowing it to "grow" in positive ways.

One way research shows we can increase levels of BDNF is through physical exercise. Levels of BDNF rise after exercise and have also been shown to counteract anxiety and depression in animal studies (Sleiman et al. 2016). Your exercise routine should be customized to your needs and preferences. Whether it's a fifteen-minute walk every day, a dance class, a Pilates class, or going to the gym, make sure that you don't overexert yourself. While many people benefit from the "runner's high" of endorphins, some trauma survivors may find exercise triggering because it raises cortisol, the stress hormone. Start with gentle exercise and go from there. Find a routine that works best for you and your brain as it's healing.

Time in Nature

As you learned earlier in the book, toxic relationships can cause dysfunction in our stress hormones. Connecting with nature can counteract some of these effects. Studies show that connecting and grounding yourself in nature can lower cortisol levels, enhance mood, and relieve stress (Ewert & Chang 2018). You can access nature in a variety of ways: gardening, taking walks by a river or in a beautiful natural park, picnicking, or walking on the earth barefoot, a practice known as "earthing."

Acupuncture

Acupuncture is an ancient Chinese healing method that uses needles to target twelve primary and eight secondary points that regulate energy flow throughout the body. These energy points are known as meridians and are said to relieve numerous emotional and physical ailments. A recent review of animal and clinical studies reveals that acupuncture may outperform pharmacotherapy treatment when it comes to improving scores on measures of PTSD (Tang et al. 2023). Acupuncture has been shown to help ease core PTSD symptoms and has been shown to reduce anxiety, depression, and fear responses, while improving sleep (Engel et al. 2014; Kwon, Lee, & Kim 2021).

Acupuncture may help treat PTSD by regulating the structure and elements of several brain areas, such as the hippocampus, amygdala, and prefrontal cortex, all of which can be affected negatively by chronic emotional trauma (Tang et al. 2023). It can also support the neuroendocrine system, the HPA axis, and signaling pathways that reduce fear and promote neuron growth.

Animal-Assisted Interventions

Working with animals can be soothing for your nervous system. Psychologists note that they have seen as high as an 82-percent reduction in PTSD symptoms due to animal-assisted interventions (Mims & Waddell 2016). Such interventions can potentially reduce fear, anxiety, and social isolation, as you are able to communicate and express your emotions with animals in a way that does not require having to speak directly about your traumas (Hediger et al. 2021). This can promote healing, processing, modeling of boundaries, empathy, mutual nurturing, and connection in a low-pressure environment, increasing interpersonal trust and healthy attachments.

Whether it's working with a trained therapist or incorporating pets into your lifestyle, the support and unconditional love of animals can potentially ease trauma, anxiety, and depression depending on your unique needs. Animals promote healthy attachment, giving you a safe support system after trauma. Numerous studies show that contact with humans can also benefit the endocrine functioning in animals, managing *their* stress response and sympathetic nervous system as well (Fine, Beck, & Ng 2019). It's a win-win situation for all.

Massage Therapy

One way to counteract the biochemical addiction survivors experience in abusive relationships is by incorporating "safe touch" by a professional. Research reveals that massage therapy can actually help lower cortisol levels while boosting serotonin and dopamine, enhancing your mood; it can also decrease depression, anxiety, irritability, and other trauma-related symptoms (Field et al. 2005; Collinge et al. 2013). If you feel comfortable using massage therapy, it can be a healing part of your self-care routine and can combat the biochemical addiction you develop to the narcissist.

Music Therapy

In music therapy, the use of music under the guidance of a therapist helps patients validate and express their emotions, process their experiences, and regulate their nervous system. A review of the literature shows that music therapy has the ability to target the hyperactive amygdala in PTSD and activate the hippocampus and prefrontal cortex, assisting in learning, memory, decision-making, emotion regulation, and even neurogenesis. Soothing, calming, and rhythmic music without lyrics tend to reduce heart rate, blood pressure, and stress-related hormones the most (Pant et al. 2022). Even if you do not attend music therapy, you can make use of this information by listening to calming relaxation music regularly or attending "sound baths" where you lie down in a comfortable position while being inundated with sound waves that induce relaxation (Goldsby & Goldsby 2020).

Steps to Break a Trauma Bond

Here are nine major steps most survivors can take to begin breaking the trauma bond to the narcissist. Targeted exercises follow each step, but you can do any of them no matter which step you are on. You can also download these exercises at http://www.newharbinger.com/53561.

1. Identify Negative and Manipulative Traits

At the start of the relationship, the narcissistic abuser may have been charming and used tactics such as love bombing—excessive contact, flattery, attention, and affection—to set themselves apart from other potential partners. They did this because they understood they could not win you over with their authentic self. They may have known you had other possible options than them and viewed you as "out of their league" in various ways. Consider that many narcissists are attracted to partners they deem "special and unique," showing them off like trophies and benefiting from their association with them. This need to associate with "special and unique" people is *literally* part of the *DSM-5* diagnostic criteria for narcissistic personality disorder!

They then slowly but surely erode your sense of self-confidence and self-respect through manipulation, demeaning comments, degradation, jealousy induction, and devaluation to maintain control over you and isolate you so you begin to see them as the "prize" to be won over. In order to break the trauma bond, you have to shatter your sense of the narcissist's illusion of false desirability created by the biochemical and psychological addiction of toxic love. Their manipulation has trained you to see yourself as "below" them, when in reality, you surpass them in many ways. *That is why they targeted you in the first place.*

Now it's time to take the narcissist off the pedestal and instead of allowing yourself to be devalued by them, mentally devalue *them*. This is not about being cruel; it is about being factual and in touch with reality. Rather than turning to the self-blame and criticism they have conditioned you to engage in, start identifying the negative qualities (both internal and external) that make the narcissist an undesirable partner for you and for other empathic people. This helps you understand that you are not truly missing out on anything and that they will never change, nor will they treat any future partner better.

Questions you can ask yourself might include: What negative qualities did you initially dislike about their personality, appearance, interests, hobbies, and demeanor? What will you *not* miss about the narcissist once they're gone? What can you do once you're free of them that you couldn't do before? What will you be free to do, feel, and think? How confident will you be? What burdens can you now let go of? What thoughts and triggers will you no longer be haunted by on a daily basis? What special occasions will no longer be sabotaged or tainted by their presence?

It's helpful to remember that the narcissist has betrayed you in many ways. You are allowed to honor your true feelings about them, so do not agonize over being ruthlessly honest when thinking about their harmful traits and the destructive impact their behavior has had on your life. After all, they did not hold back from depicting you in vile ways with falsehoods and projections. The best act of self-compassion is to now center yourself in the truth about them. This will empower you to see the toxic people in your life accurately rather than through the rose-colored lenses of the love-bombing and devaluation cycle. It will ultimately remind you that being free from them is a blessing and will incentivize you to cut ties with more fervor. The following exercise can help you with this process.

EXERCISE: Reconnect with the Facts to Resist Gaslighting

You've undoubtedly experienced feeling like your perception of reality and your self-image were distorted and questioned throughout the relationship. Here are some writing prompts to help you reconnect with the facts and resist gaslighting.

- How often do you try to fix or defend against your abuser's perception of you? How could you validate yourself instead without the abuser's input? For example, could you write down incidents where people told you that you were kind and caring, or moments that signal how accomplished and successful you are, if these were traits they tried to convince you that you didn't have?

- The narcissist has engaged in distorted thinking throughout the relationship to make you feel like you were the one to blame. Write down three accusations or labels the narcissist has given you that you feel were unwarranted based on the facts (e.g., "They told me I was insecure/jealous/controlling").

- Add a rebuttal to these three accusations. For example: "The narcissist told me I was jealous and possessive, but they were actually the one who was checking up on me 24/7 during the love-bombing phase." This helps ground you in the reality of their gaslighting and reconnects you with the facts.

EXERCISE: Are You Making Excuses?

Here are some writing prompts you can do in your journal or by using the worksheet available online.

It's common to want to make sense of the behavior of our partners. That makes us human! But sometimes, we hang on to rationalizations that aren't accurate. We may even do so out of habit, not realizing we're making excuses for actions that aren't acceptable. Read the rationalizations below and consider whether this is a rationalization you have made. Then, read the sample reframings. In your journal, add your own reframings. This exercise will help you reframe your thinking to better reflect reality and allow you to get in touch with your valid anger.

Rationalization #1: They had an abusive childhood. They are lashing out. Hurt people hurt people. I have to be compassionate and understanding.

Sample Reframings

There are people who had abusive childhoods who do not go out of their way to harm innocent people. Trauma may explain some behaviors, but abuse is still a choice.

Not all abusive partners have experienced childhood maltreatment. Research indicates that parental overvaluation can lead to narcissistic traits. Empirically, parental maltreatment or lack of parental warmth does not predict narcissistic traits in research studies. Narcissists may come from a variety of childhood backgrounds, and while that may provide a better understanding of some of their behaviors now, that doesn't excuse them.

Rationalization #2: They didn't know what they were doing. They're frustrated and just can't control their emotions.

Sample Reframings

They know how to control their behavior around witnesses and key stakeholders.

When I am distant from them, they seem to draw me back into the cycle with the sweet behavior they presented in the beginning, which means they know how to control their behavior when it gets them what they want.

If they know they have issues with aggression, frustration tolerance, or anger, they can go to therapy and choose to get help. Yet despite receiving feedback indicating their behavior is harmful, they choose not to.

Rationalization #3: They're addicted to substances. They can't help themselves when they act out.

Sample Reframings

Not everyone who has substance abuse issues is abusive to others. A deeper core lack of empathy may be the problem here.

If they do have substance abuse issues, they can choose to seek help instead of lashing out at others.

Consider the "Dark Reality" of Staying in the Relationship

You might fear "missing out" on the narcissist and may romanticize certain aspects of the relationship that keep you tethered to them. Now, let's look at the other side. What will happen if you continue to stay and engage in the relationship?

What will you continue to lose emotionally, financially, and health-wise? What burdens will overwhelm you?

What opportunities will slip by because you were too focused on the narcissist to work on yourself or your goals?

Identify "Survival" Sources That Are Keeping You Stuck

Reality distortion helps keep us safe and can be an evolutionarily adaptive response to keep us connected to resources that help us stay alive. What survival mechanisms meant to protect you are also keeping the relationship intact?

What are ways you can use other resources besides the narcissist to meet this need for survival? (e.g., Can you pick up another job to build some savings so you're not entirely reliant on the narcissist? Can you speak to a lawyer about custody and divorce proceedings? Can you work on your fear of abandonment in therapy so that you don't abandon yourself?)

2. Connect with Your Authentic Anger at Being Violated and the Reality of the Abuse

You may have noticed that your narcissistic partner discourages any expressions of anger from you, gaslighting you into believing that you are bitter or crazy if you ever speak up against their mistreatment. That is because your anger is actually a very powerful emotion—one that has the power to break the trauma bond in ways other emotions cannot. The real reason narcissistic and psychopathic individuals feel so compelled to punish you for healthy expressions of anger is because they know that if you got in touch with it, you would be more likely to ground yourself in the reality of the violations that are occurring and be able to leave them with far more confidence in yourself and your perceptions. That is why they demonize any valid anger you express toward them and admonish you for "not letting things go," rather than acknowledging that you're having legitimate reactions to their inhumane cruelty. After all, if they didn't want you to bring up the past, they shouldn't have repeated it in the first place.

When you are clouded in the mental fog of abuse, you're more likely to rationalize the red flags to survive what you're experiencing. Anger cuts through this mental fog, allowing you to defend and protect yourself against predators. When you connect with the natural sense of disgust and outrage you feel toward someone who has betrayed you, you are that much closer to overcoming conflicting thoughts and emotions that keep you tied to your abuser. The key to honoring the valid anger you feel toward the narcissist isn't necessarily about confronting them with it or using it in destructive ways, but rather harnessing this anger strategically to detach from them. You can channel this anger productively to fuel you toward cutting ties with them, going "no contact," and protecting yourself in healthy ways. You may also wish to document and keep a list of abusive incidents to remind you of what has occurred so you can validate yourself and connect with your anger. The following exercises will help you get in touch with your anger, recount the betrayals you have experienced to validate that anger, and stop making excuses for the abuser.

EXERCISE: Reconnect with Your Anger

Here are some writing prompts you can do in your journal or by using the worksheet available online.

- Write down at least five incidents when the narcissist tried to punish you for experiencing anger and times you suppressed your own anger to maintain the relationship.

- What would you feel organically in these instances if you didn't fear losing the narcissist?

- As you look at each incident with fresh eyes, breathe and ground yourself using box breathing (see next page). Allow yourself to slowly experience some of the outrage, sadness, or suppressed emotions that you prevented yourself from experiencing during those times. Work with a therapist if this is too overwhelming and use your anger to detach from your romanticized notions of who you thought the narcissist was, and connect to their true nature instead. Anger can help you move through the breakup with a narcissist with more relief.

- Brainstorm how you can express or use the anger you're experiencing constructively. For example, can you channel this anger into a physical outlet like jogging, kickboxing, or dancing? Can you write an uncensored, unsent letter to your toxic partner that allows you to disclose everything you feel without shame or self-judgment?

- After processing this anger in therapy, how might you channel these experiences for the greater good or higher good? Some survivors find great relief in using their anger to fuel their passions and dreams—as motivation to go back to school, write their first book, pursue their dream career, or supercharge their finances. Some survivors become advocates for spreading awareness, or even become therapists, lawyers, changemakers, researchers, and experts themselves in order to educate the public on the dynamics of abuse and healing. When anger is honored and processed constructively, it can be an amazing tool to uplevel your life and also give back to the community.

Box Breathing

Box breathing helps you return your breathing back to its normal rhythm after your body goes through fight-or-flight mode. To do box breathing, inhale slowly for a count of four seconds. Hold the breath for four seconds. Prolong your exhale for a count of four seconds. Repeat this process four times until you feel sufficiently more relaxed.

You can find the guided audio for box breathing at http://www.newhar binger.com/53561.

EXERCISE: Validate Yourself

Notice what you are feeling and thinking at this very moment about the toxic relationship you're in or have recently detached from. In your journal, write what you feel in your body (the parts of your body that have tension), the automatic thoughts that arise, and any emotion you may currently be struggling with. This helps you acknowledge and honor your emotions and build nonjudgmental awareness of them. For example, you may notice anger that tries to come up, but you usually suppress it due to the trauma bond. Instead, ask yourself why the anger or despair is there and what need isn't being met. Brainstorm healthy ways to meet this need and send yourself compassion at this time.

EXERCISE: Track Both Betrayal and Self-Betrayal

Here are some writing prompts you can do in your journal or the worksheet available online.

- Identify the ways in which the narcissist has betrayed your trust and basic human rights.

- Also identify incidents of "self-betrayal"—where you found yourself foregoing your own boundaries to cater to the narcissist out of fear, obligation, or guilt.

- They have desensitized you to a new normal. It's time to re-sensitize yourself. What are the violations of the relationship that are absolutely abhorrent, abnormal, and not acceptable?

- What types of things could you peacefully do before this relationship that you cannot do now? How do you feel about yourself now that you would never imagine feeling before?

- How have you acted out of character because of this toxic person?

3. Disrupt Your Usual Patterns and Habits While Leveling Up

Trauma bonds cause victims to develop certain patterns of thinking, feeling, and behaving that are used to cope with the trauma of the relationship. In a toxic relationship with a narcissist, you've likely developed endless compulsive habits. It's important to begin interrupting and disrupting these patterns, which center the abuser as the focus of your existence, and instead create "periods of peace" away from your abuser so you can learn to live life without them. One of the most productive ways you can do this is by replacing your usual self-destructive patterns associated with the narcissist with an activity that allows you to "level up"—an activity serving your self-care, healing, career goals, mental health, or physical fitness. This has the added benefit of nourishing your well-being over time, heightening your confidence, and reminding you that you do deserve better. It's one of the first steps to creating a life you look forward to living away from the narcissist. These new healthy habits need to become ingrained in your everyday behavior. Just like you developed toxic habits, you can rewire your brain with new, empowering habits to replace them.

For example, if you have a habit of always contacting the narcissist when you're in distress, even if they were the cause of the stressful situation, you might start to replace that habit with taking a daily walk. This will boost your fitness and mood, allowing you to "level up" as you detach from the trauma bond. If the toxic person is giving you the silent treatment or devaluing you and you have a pattern of chasing them, use these silent treatments as an opportunity to detach from them and return back to yourself by engaging in a new or old hobby or working toward one of your goals. You can also make use of this specific time period to engage in "reality checking" about their abusive patterns and replenish your self-care practices.

If you tend to check up on your abusive partner because you suspect they're up to their usual schemes, you can disrupt that habit by using the time to engage in some form of self-care that will replenish you, such as immersing yourself in nature, meditating, doing yoga, or anything else that centers and grounds you. If you have a pattern of texting them every morning or constantly throughout the day, you can interrupt this pattern by texting them later in the day and using that extra time to jog, read, or connect with a supportive friend. You might use this extra time to search for additional resources on narcissism and visit online support forums centered around abuse recovery.

If you have a pattern of always attempting to overexplain yourself and your emotions in response to their gaslighting, you can start to break that pattern by walking away from arguments before they escalate and spending that time journaling about the incident and how it made you feel. This has the double benefit of resisting their gaslighting attempts while bringing back your power and giving you the space for a reprieve. The following exercises will help you examine your unhealthy habits and replace them with healthy ones, examine how your behavior strengthens the trauma bond, and shift your self-blame into self-compassion. You can also find guided healing meditations to recover from the effects of gaslighting, pathological envy, stonewalling, and trauma bonds at http://www.newharbinger.com/53561.

EXERCISE: What Are Your Daily Habits Related to the Trauma Bond?

Here are some writing prompts you can do in your journal or the worksheet available online.

- What are the daily compulsive habits you engage in that keep you connected to your abuser? (For example, "I always text my abuser as soon as I wake up" or "I check in with my abuser throughout the day or look at their social media.")

- What are a few activities you could use to replace those habits with a fruitful or productive outlet that will benefit your healing, self-care, or goals?

Sample Replacement Activities

- Instead of checking social media, I can exercise, go for a walk in nature, run on the treadmill, use social media productively by looking at positive content only, use that time and energy to meditate and do breathing exercises.

- Instead of contacting them, I can write in my journal, write a letter that I don't send instead of giving them the reaction they're looking for, or contact someone trustworthy and supportive.

EXERCISE: Shifting from Self-Blame to Self-Compassion

Here are some writing prompts you can do in your journal or on the worksheet available online.

Give back responsibility to the narcissist for what they did to you instead of engaging in self-blame. Create a two-column chart in your journal and write your self-blaming thoughts in the first column. Get curious about these self-blaming thoughts and gently interrogate them. In the second column, provide evidence against your self-blaming thoughts. Look at the sample chart below for some ideas.

Self-Blaming Thought	Evidence Against Self-Blaming Thought
I am so insecure and jealous.	They chronically tried to make me feel insecure because they didn't want me to leave them or know I could do better. They used jealousy induction to distort my self-esteem and self-concept.
It's my fault because I should have known better!	Abusers target different people because of their own lack of empathy and entitlement. Their manipulation tactics tend to bypass the logical brain and prey on the vulnerabilities of others.

The manipulator *chose* to take advantage and that manipulation is their responsibility, not yours. Unlike a loving, healthy person, they chose to harm someone who has already been harmed rather than help them. Those are their actions, not yours. Talk back to your inner critic and use thought substitution and self-compassion. For example, if you start thinking, *I am such a bad person. Why did I do this to myself?* you may substitute this thought with, *I've been through so much. I am so strong to have survived. It may feel hard now, but I know I can get through this. I am worthy of healing.*

Evaluate beliefs about your locus of control (the control you feel over your life and how you tend to attribute the cause of events). Do you believe you were the one who "caused" the abuser's behavior? Are there other factors you're not identifying that may be out of your control? For example,

an abuser will act aggressively to get what they want because they feel entitled to it. That is not your fault and has nothing to do with you.

When self-blame comes up, turn back to self-compassion. Speak to
yourself as if you were your own best friend, or as if you were a parent to
your inner child. If you were comforting and soothing someone you truly
loved, how would you do so? How can you be more gentle with yourself? For
example, you might tell yourself soothing, validating things like, "I know
it's so painful and so unfair. You never deserved this treatment." You might
let yourself cry and hug yourself, or wrap yourself in a warm blanket.

4. Invite Novelty into Your Behavior and Thinking Patterns

Incorporating safe practices and activities that are new and empowering can be helpful when breaking a trauma bond. When the brain is
accustomed to constant trauma and chaos, it doesn't see a way out. It
seeks to trap you in the same patterns because it's familiar, even if it's
dangerous. According to neuroscientist Dr. Tara Swart, the brain is
energy efficient (Dixon 2022). When a thought is repeated a sufficient
amount of times or holds a heavy weight of emotional intensity, it becomes
connected to thick neural pathways, making it easier for chemicals and
electrical signals to pass through. That is why the brain takes the path of
least resistance, resorting to the same thinking patterns and behavioral
responses that it's accustomed to, time and time again, when not sufficiently challenged.

The brain tends to fear new things because it can perceive them as a
threat; the amygdala and hippocampus often work together to bring up
negative memories and thoughts whenever we are faced with the unfamil-
iar. So when we are accustomed to the highs and lows of crazy-making
relationships, it can feel overwhelming and scary to venture out to the
unknown comfort of solitude or being in a state of peace and joy.

While these neural pathways cannot be "deleted," they *can* be over-
written with new ones. That is why inviting novel practices and instilling
healthier habits in our lives, which will continue to rewire the brain,

allows us to automate good habits over time so that the brain finally takes the path of least resistance toward healthier habits instead. So, for example, if after a breakup with a narcissist, you develop a pattern of meditating or doing yoga and spending more time healing on your own, your brain and its patterns will become accustomed to the pattern of healing rather than self-destructive relationships.

Inviting novel behaviors and practices incrementally and with care, adapted to your level of safety and comfort, is essential. These do not have to be drastic changes; they can be as minor as going to a new coffee shop where you're exposed to new faces, learning some words from a new language, or reading a book about a topic you've rarely explored. Or they can be as major as taking a class in a subject you're not knowledgeable about, traveling to a country you've never been to, or trying a new fitness activity like jiu-jitsu. Not only will these novel practices replace the dopamine rush your brain gets from toxic relationships with a healthier outlet, but they will also keep your brain growing and expanding—something that is essential for a healthy brain, especially one that has experienced neural atrophy from trauma. In the following exercise, you'll discover ways to work with your neurotransmitters and hormones to train your brain away from toxic love and toward greater healing.

EXERCISE: Working with the Brain

As you learned in chapter 3, a toxic trauma bond can be very addictive because of how biochemically attached we become to the narcissist. Essential to breaking the trauma bond is making your brain work *for* you rather than *against* you during the healing journey. Let's revisit the list of neurotransmitters and hormones involved and examples for activities that serve these in healthier ways. In your journal, write down your own activities list customized to you.

> **Serotonin.** Serotonin can affect your mood and willpower. To boost and balance serotonin levels, take long sunny walks in nature, engage in a gratitude practice (which boosts both serotonin and dopamine), and relive happy memories.

Dopamine. Dopamine can affect your focus and motivation. To increase dopamine, set long-term goals and reward yourself as you take baby steps toward these goals, engage in "novelty" (learn a new language, take a class in a new subject, or travel to a new place) on a weekly basis, and engage in physical exercise.

Cortisol. The stress of a toxic relationship inevitably causes cortisol levels to go haywire. High levels of cortisol can lead to intense levels of inflammation throughout the body, cause weight gain and high blood pressure, and increase irritability and depression. To lower cortisol levels, do light to moderate gentle exercise, engage in positive social interactions with trusted loved ones, do deep breathing, or get a relaxing massage.

5. Connect with Your Uniqueness and Positive Qualities to Build Healthy Pride

A relationship with a narcissist creates not only destructive habits but also destructive beliefs about ourselves, the world, and other people. You may have noticed that when you're in a toxic relationship, other aspects of your life fall apart. Many survivors attest to this sense of misfortune that entered their lives when the narcissist began manipulating them. This is no coincidence. A toxic relationship devalues your self-concept to the point where you start to shrink and feel small in different facets of your life. When the narcissist elevates you and places you on a pedestal, you feel on top of the world because they encourage a beautiful self-concept, even if it existed prior to their arrival.

On the other hand, when they devalue you, your self-concept becomes associated with the negative projections of their own undesirable traits onto you. The adversity they put you through trains your brain to expect chaos and to view yourself in a distorted way. This can leave you feeling more helpless in other aspects of your life, such as your general self-confidence, friendships, finances, and mental health—it's like a massive domino effect. That's why it's important to rewrite your self-concept while healing from the trauma bond, because the narcissist has essentially "hijacked" your self-concept to make you believe that you embody qualities and traits that are actually opposite of who you really are.

When you already have self-confidence in your positive traits, you are less susceptible to love bombing. When you have a healthy ego that is invested in protecting you from harm and danger, you're more likely to fight back and resist a narcissist degrading you, even as you're being trauma bonded. The ego helps you remember what you deserve and the fact that you're worthy. Connect to your healthy sense of ego by validating the legitimate anger you experience when violated—this anger is what can help you detach from the narcissist and remind you of what they have put you through, bypassing the usual rationalization and minimization (remember step 2?).

The narcissist, society, and religious traditions may have convinced you that acknowledging your strengths is "egotistical." Ironic, right? It's actually narcissists who need to work on their ego, not you. The narcissist deliberately targets your strengths to keep you compliant.

You may not be at the part of your journey yet where you are grounded in self-validation. That's okay. You will get there. For now, it's time to remind yourself of what makes you unique, special, and irreplaceable—what makes breaking up with you a loss and what makes being free from the narcissist a gain. An abusive relationship with a narcissist trains you to always compare yourself to others and forget who you are. It's time to remind yourself that you have no competition.

Treat yourself like royalty—someone who should not settle for less. You'll begin to notice that as your self-concept changes, the way you treat yourself transforms too: on a day where you may usually neglect yourself, you find yourself dressing up and going outdoors to enjoy the sunshine; where once you spent hours in bed, you now find yourself making plans and taking steps toward your goals. It might feel uncomfortable at first, but eventually, you will learn to put yourself on a pedestal and mentally devalue narcissistic people in ways that make them undesirable to you. You will no longer feel the need to have them in your life or crave their validation because you will have a stronger sense of your own power and inner validation. The following exercises will strengthen your self-concept and teach you how to resist the abuser's distortions and projections.

EXERCISE: Creating a Strong Self-Concept

Here are some writing prompts you can do in your journal or using the worksheet available online.

Create a chart in your journal that looks like the one below. Then, take an inventory of the negative beliefs and thoughts the narcissist instilled in you and write these in the first column. It can help to work with a therapist in doing this if you get heavily triggered by bringing up these beliefs. In the second column, write down the healthier beliefs you prefer to instill in yourself. In the third column, write down the evidence you've witnessed or feedback you've received that supports this healthy belief. Look at the sample chart below for some ideas.

Negative Beliefs Instilled in Me	Healthier Beliefs I Instill in Myself	Evidence for Healthy Belief
They made me believe I was crazy, that I wasn't capable, and that I was oversensitive.	I am so capable and competent. I have great instincts. I am intelligent and goal-driven.	I graduated top of my class. I ran two successful businesses. My friends comment on how ambitious, intuitive, and friendly I am.

Each time you find yourself ruminating over one of the old beliefs the narcissist instilled in you, get into the habit of gradually replacing it with an affirmation that strengthens the new belief you want to instill. Gently notice the anxiety that comes up when you make a mistake, but refuse to add to the narrative that it means you're incompetent. By rewiring your brain toward the healthy belief, you will also shape the actions you take in your life. For example, believing you're competent and capable can give you more motivation to go after dreams and goals you may have felt doubtful about pursuing otherwise. In your journal, make a list of the affirmations you will use.

EXERCISE: Resisting Projection and Distortion

Here are some writing prompts you can do in your journal or using the worksheet available online.

Create a chart in your journal that looks like the one below. Then, make a list of the activities, interests, hobbies, and traits that the narcissist demeaned in you. Next to each, write down the positive benefits you gained from these activities and assets. Then, write down what may have threatened the narcissist about this activity. Finally, write down a list of positive feedback others have given you about that trait or behavior. Look at the sample chart below for some ideas.

Activities, Hobbies, and Interests That Were Demeaned	Positive Benefits I Gained	What Was Threatening to Them	Positive Feedback I Received from Others
They told me going back to school was a waste of time and that I am not smart enough to get a degree.	I enjoyed going back to school because I love to learn and getting a degree heightens my earning potential.	They did not want me to go back to school because it challenged their control over me and they were pathologically envious.	I have gotten amazing feedback from my professors about my work.

EXERCISE: Deprogram Destructive Conditioning

As you learned earlier, destructive conditioning is when the narcissist conditions you to associate your strengths, achievements, and positive moments with punishment so you are less likely to engage in these activities or pursue your goals. To deprogram destructive conditioning, here are some writing prompts you can do in your journal or using the worksheet available online.

- Write down the incidents of joy, celebration, and milestones that the narcissist interfered with (e.g., "My narcissistic partner tried to sabotage my graduation by making snide comments about my intelligence during my graduation party").

- Write down an activity you could engage in to celebrate the event and remember positive encouragement from others (e.g., "I can look back at the photos and videos of my graduation and reread compliments and congratulations from my loved ones on social media").

- Next, write down any intrusive and automatic thoughts that come up related to the narcissist's demeaning comments or behaviors toward you. Pick a few images and affirmations and write down multiple options to "oppose" this intrusive thought. (For example, if your intrusive thought is, "I can't do anything right," start to replace this intrusive thought with, "I've achieved so many amazing things," paired with an image of your favorite accomplishment.)

EXERCISE: Self-Validate and Set Healthy Boundaries

Here are some writing prompts you can do in your journal or using the worksheet available online.

The narcissist has fed you distortions about who you are and what you're capable of, leading to erosion of not just your sense of self but also your boundaries and standards. It's vital that you rework these distortions to reconnect with who you really are. The following prompts will guide you to rethink the way you've been taught to think about yourself, the relationship, and your right to have boundaries due to the narcissist's manipulation.

Learn to Set Boundaries

I created the following acronym for setting boundaries. Copy the list into your journal. Then, next to each action, brainstorm and write down small and big ways you can set healthier boundaries. For example, next to "Believe in your own worth," you might write something like, "I will do positive affirmations to remind myself of my inherent value." Next to "Dealbreakers," you might list the red flags you will no longer tolerate in dating and relationships.

Believe in your own worth.

Own your agency.

Understand your core values.

Name your nonnegotiables.

Dealbreakers.

Assert without apologies.

Reinforce and repeat if challenged.

Implement practically and safely.

Exit when not respected.

Save yourself and prioritize your self-care.

Ground Yourself in Your Own Mind

When in doubt, turn within. Gently turn the focus off what the narcissist is doing, feeling, and thinking and back onto what you are doing, feeling, and thinking. Answer the following prompts in your journal.

- What are *you* excited about?

- How do *you* feel?

- What goals do *you* want to accomplish?

- What milestones are *you* trying to achieve?

Identify Childhood Experiences You May Be Repeating

Identify early childhood incidents of devaluation, abuse, neglect, rejection, and betrayal you experienced. What incidents seem to be "recreated" in adulthood? For example, when you were young, you may have witnessed explosive arguments between your parents. How does that reflect in the way you become entangled with toxic partners in arguments and feel unable to detach? These childhood experiences may be hindering your ability to set healthy boundaries.

6. Surround Yourself with Healthy Communities

Your narcissistic partner isolated you from the healthy, positive feedback that kept you grounded in your sense of self. Now it's time to remember this positive feedback and surround yourself with support. Make a list of all the personality traits, talents, skills, and physical assets you have been complimented on by healthy, empathic people. Include your own acknowledgment of your strengths. As you break the trauma bond, also remember what the narcissist claimed they disliked about you or tried to actively sabotage. Then, in the process of breaking the trauma bond or after you've safely exited the relationship, *do more of that*. What narcissists claim are your weaknesses are actually your strengths. The following exercises will help you break free from the abuser's destructive conditioning.

EXERCISE: Slowly Rejoin Healthy Activities

Here are some writing prompts you can do in your journal or by using the worksheet that's available online.

The narcissist has conditioned you to avoid the healthy and positive things that make you happy. Slowly exposing yourself to your former, healthy activities can help you rebuild your sense of efficacy, resilience, and confidence in your capabilities.

What places, things, or activities do you avoid as a result of your relationship with the narcissist? For example, did you stop going out with friends because the narcissist punished you every time you did? Did you stop working on a project or goal because the narcissist lashed out enviously when you began receiving a steady income or a job promotion?

Brainstorm how to slowly expose yourself to these activities again in a healthy way. For example, perhaps you take a class to build knowledge or call a trusted friend to reconnect with over lunch.

7. Find Trauma-Informed Professional Support

As we discussed earlier in this chapter, there are many diverse healing modalities available to you as a trauma survivor. Healing from the trauma bond is usually most effective when you have a safe space to process your experiences with a trauma-informed professional. Ensure that the therapist you choose is well-versed in personality disorders, is validating, and has a deep understanding of trauma responses and the effects of trauma on the brain. Speak to your therapist about their skill set and training in DBT and EMDR, as these can potentially be helpful tools they can use to guide you on your journey.

8. Heal Your Inner Child and Connect with Inner Parts

When breaking the trauma bond, we have to understand both our inner child as well as our inner parts that have been maintaining the trauma bond. Clinical psychologist Dr. Richard Schwartz developed the internal family systems model to better identify the different self-states he has witnessed in his clients (Brenner, Schwartz, & Becker 2023). Although each person has a core, compassionate "Self," the internal family systems model posits that we develop other "inner parts" that are different from this core "Self." These inner parts can be shaped by our childhood experiences and traumas. When these inner parts are healthy, unburdened, and able to contribute to our well-being and survival *without* using maladaptive strategies, the internal system can be led successfully by the core "Self," the compassionate, calm, centered, connected, and grounded self we all have within us. Each inner part wants something positive for the core "Self" but may use maladaptive strategies to achieve their goals. These inner parts can reveal themselves through behaviors, thoughts, emotions, images, and sensations, and provide feedback to the "Self" that guides the decisions the "Self" makes. When the inner parts are burdened with traumas and triggers, they can act out in extreme ways that harm us, even though their intentions are usually to defend, protect, and guide us back to safety.

There tends to be three main types of inner parts: "exiles," "managers," and "firefighters."

Exiles. Younger parts are known as "exile" parts that carry the shame, wounds, and fear of early childhood traumas. Exile inner parts are especially vulnerable and fragile; they may seek validation, reassurance, and comfort, and feel a need to tell their story and have it heard. Exile inner parts can hold an intense desire to avoid abandonment and attach to the narcissist out of fear of being abandoned again and having to confront their childhood trauma alone. These parts can become especially trauma bonded to the abuser and come to view the abuser as a "rescuer" figure even though the abuser is also the source of their present pain and trauma. Since the narcissistic or psychopathic abuser creates a cycle of hurt-and-rescue and intermittent reinforcement with their victims, the exile inner parts may be severely triggered into making frantic attempts to avoid abandonment and seek validation from the abuser. This can cause you to return to the relationship repeatedly, even when it becomes unhealthy and destructive.

Managers. Inner parts known as "managers" can cause us to maintain control over our relationships through micromanaging and caretaking. Managers are the protector inner parts that proactively and preemptively attempt to control potentially triggering situations to prevent the pain of exiles from being experienced in the first place. They try to shield the younger parts and their wounds from being exposed to the perceived dangers of the world. Managers operate through perfectionism, caretaking, overachieving, constantly striving toward goals, people-pleasing, codependency, and engaging in hypercritical or aggressive behaviors toward others in order to control them. In a relationship with a narcissist, your manager inner parts may try to repress core wounds from surfacing by trying to control the narcissist's behaviors or by engaging in self-blame. They may take on a caretaker role with the narcissist to try to "nurse" or educate the narcissist back into being an empathic person, an effort that often proves fruitless. You might also micromanage and hypercriticize the narcissist in order to try to "prevent" the abuse from occurring.

Manager inner parts may also cause you to excessively try to fix or improve *yourself* in an attempt to avoid the narcissist's abuse, overexplain or defend yourself, or engage in people pleasing or fawning to maintain the relationship so the pain of losing the narcissist doesn't disrupt other aspects of your life. Due to your manager inner parts, you may also be pushed to distract yourself from what is happening in the relationship with overachieving or striving toward goals, as you are unwilling to confront the reality of the abuse that is occurring. Unfortunately, this means all your efforts are put into surviving the relationship rather than detaching from it, which makes it more difficult to break a trauma bond and exit dangerous situations. Some survivors of narcissists may also have manager inner parts that opt out of relationships altogether to avoid the risk of any pain at all.

Firefighters. These are also protector inner parts that react immediately to the pain of exile inner parts by engaging in addictions and distractions. "Firefighter" inner parts are like the emergency responders. When they sense trouble is afoot, these inner parts immediately "douse out fires" by dissociating and distracting with addictive behaviors, thus shielding exile younger parts from being triggered by numbing the pain. When you are with a narcissistic or psychopathic individual, your firefighter inner parts can push you to dissociate from the abuse and engage in extreme behaviors to numb out and "freeze" in the midst of all the pain and chaos. They could also persuade you to overindulge in the pleasures the relationship intermittently provides (such as with love bombing and sex) while dissociating from the actual abuse. This creates an even more powerful biochemical bond to the abuser. However, by avoiding the pain, these actions can worsen your trauma symptoms and can result in you denying the truth about the abuse present in the relationship, thus strengthening your trauma bond to the narcissist.

There is hope for integrating and empowering the inner parts to work together to reach their goals in healthier ways. As you work with your manager parts to release more control and turn to self-agency and self-care, as you help the firefighter parts gradually confront and process the pain without numbing it out, and as you aid exile parts in healing their wounds and unburdening their sense of shame or guilt from childhood, they usually feel safer and more secure and shift into more empowering roles. Without the overprotection of managers and firefighters, exiles can now confront their authentic pain with better coping methods without feeling as overwhelmed. They are able to experience the discomfort and distress of detaching from a toxic person without attempting to avoid abandonment and strengthening the trauma bond to the narcissist. They feel more open to finding validation and comfort in those who show them true empathy, kindness, and compassion. They discover a safe haven at long last, both within themselves and with empathic others. They can tell their stories without having to feel silenced or punished by a narcissist or other toxic people.

When all these inner parts work together and communicate in healthy ways, the "Self" can emerge as a compassionate, calm, creative, curious, and connected leader that incorporates feedback from the unburdened inner parts and guides the internal system back to the safety, nurturance, and well-being it always deserves. Integrating and communicating with your inner parts can help you understand which ones may be dominant in your relationship with the narcissist and may be working against you, running the show when it comes to the trauma bond. "Speaking" to those inner parts, with the help of a therapist, can allow you to identify the behaviors of each part and better meet its needs without engaging in self-destruction by staying attached to a toxic person.

The following exercises will help you learn more about your inner parts, reduce the dissociation that the firefighters often engage in to keep you numb, and use vagus nerve exercises to help heal your nervous system so that your manager and exile inner parts feel more in control.

EXERCISE: Connect to Your Inner Parts

Here are some writing prompts you can do in your journal or by using the worksheet available online.

- What aspects of yourself seem out of character with your general personality?

- Based on the description of the different inner parts, which kind of inner part do you think you are dealing with?

- What do you think this part desires for you?

- How does it behave to obtain that goal?

- How does this inner part strengthen or weaken your trauma bond with the narcissist?

- How can you integrate this inner part in a healthier way?

Example 1

Perhaps you have an exile inner part who fears abandonment due to its core wounds, so it clings to the narcissist even when being mistreated. Perhaps its desire is to keep you feeling emotionally safe to avoid abandonment, but in reality, it keeps you in more danger. Integrating this inner part safely may include inner child work with a therapist to heal childhood wounds, or understanding that self-abandonment is also a painful form of abandonment and can often cause even deeper despair than abandonment by a toxic person.

Example 2

Maybe you have a manager inner part who tries to micromanage the narcissist's behavior toward you by overexplaining yourself, your boundaries, and your rights even though they disrespect them time and time again. The manager tries to keep you feeling in control in what is an otherwise out-of-control relationship. To take back control and agency in ways that do not involve the narcissist's validation, you could join a community of survivors who validate your experiences, or work on personal goals like enhancing your health and fitness, which will allow you to regain self-confidence and detach from the narcissist.

EXERCISE: Integrating Your Inner Parts

Here are some writing prompts you can do in your journal or using the worksheet available online.

- Evaluate your fight, flight, freeze, and fawn responses to your narcissistic partner. Which inner parts do you think are running the show here?

- You might need to grieve your inner child wounds, your pre-trauma self, the toxic relationship, and the life-course trajectory changes that occurred due to the relationship. How can you grieve while not blaming yourself?

- Remind yourself that you are an adult now, not your exile inner parts, with the ability to leave dangerous situations. How can you reassure the exile parts that you will be safe?

EXERCISE: Reducing Dissociation

As you learned earlier in the book, dissociation includes feeling detached from your body and surroundings. Here are some ways you can reduce dissociation.

- During the day, take the time to connect to your surroundings. Do breathing exercises or a short meditation.

- When in doubt, talk aloud to yourself. Ground yourself in what you are experiencing through your five senses (e.g., "I am in my room," "I am basking in the sunlight," "It's Wednesday at 4 p.m.").

- Ask yourself questions and answer them. For example, "What am I feeling today?" "I am feeling excited, energized, and productive. I have ruminating thoughts about my partner being mad at me this morning."

- Give self-encouragement. Say to yourself, "I am making progress. I am proud of myself."

- Take aligned action. What action can you take today that would make you feel a bit better? Perhaps you need to take a short walk around the neighborhood, immerse yourself in nature, or do a short meditation or breathing exercise to ground yourself in the present moment.

EXERCISE: Vagus Nerve Exercises to Calm the Stress Response

Your inner parts and triggers are most likely activating extreme stress responses because of their own particular needs and vulnerabilities. As you learned in chapter 2, the vagus nerve helps calm down the body after the fight-or-flight response has been evoked. Here are some ways you can activate the vagus nerve to help heal your nervous system. This list is also available at http://www.newharbinger.com/53561.

- **Breathing exercises.** The vagus nerve can be activated through specialized deep-breathing exercises, such as with box breathing or by breathing deeply from your diaphragm.

- **Utilize cold.** You can take cold showers, put ice cubes on your skin, splash your face with cold water, or take an ice bath to awaken the vagus nerve.

- **Side-to-side head movements.** You can activate the vagus nerve by turning your head to each side and having your eyes face the opposite direction.

- **Using sound.** Humming or singing can activate the vagus nerve.

- **Self-massage.** You can massage your vagus nerve by massaging your inner ear or the sides of your neck.

- **Exercise.** Movement can also activate the vagus nerve. Go for a walk, attend a yoga class, or engage in some interval and endurance training.

- **Meditation.** Meditation helps strengthen vagal tone and reduces fight-or-flight activity. Listen to a guided meditation online or take at least five minutes every day to sit in a quiet place and focus on your breath.

9. Go No Contact or Low Contact Depending on Your Circumstances

We know that toxic love is essentially like a drug addiction. "Rehab" is necessary for recovery. Time and space away from the abuser help the brain heal and return to your sense of self without the narcissist. In the last chapter, you will learn how to safely exit a toxic relationship with a narcissist and maintain "no contact" or "low contact" depending on your circumstances. The following grounding exercises will help you manage the anxiety and stress that may arise when you want to contact your partner (but know you shouldn't) or when you know you will have to talk to or see them (perhaps because you have children).

EXERCISE: Self-Soothing Grounding Methods

If you're finding it difficult to focus due to anxiety or other overwhelming emotions, try these methods to cognitively ground yourself (i.e., noticing and reworking your thought processes to be more mindful in the present moment). This list is also available at http://www.newharbinger.com/53561.

- Start a dialogue with yourself to disrupt the brain's tendency to downward spiral during traumatic moments. Ask yourself aloud, "Are you okay? What do you need right now?"

- Ask yourself follow-up questions and provide answers. Say, for example, "I am okay. I just need to take a break and not do anything."

- Speak to yourself compassionately and encouragingly. Say, "You're okay. You are allowed to rest. I love you."

- Ask yourself which inner parts need help. Note the "age" of certain inner parts and communicate with them about their roles, needs, and wants.

Takeaways

In this chapter, you learned about the different strategies and therapeutic tools to help you break and heal from your trauma bonds—including evidence-based therapies like DBT, EMDR, and CBT, as well as methods such as exercise, yoga, and animal-assisted intervention, to help your mind and body recover from trauma. You practiced your skills in nervous system regulation, mindfulness, leveling up, inner parts work, goal-setting, building a strong self-concept, grounding, and self-soothing through the numerous exercises provided. You should be very proud of yourself for taking these important steps to take better care of yourself and detach from toxic relationships. Next, we will revisit how to tackle manipulation, no matter what stage of the trauma-bonding cycle you may be in, and discuss how to maintain healthy boundaries in dating and relationships long term.

CHAPTER 5

Navigating Manipulation Tactics

Narcissists maintain trauma bonds through continued manipulation. You've learned about many of the manipulation tactics they use, such as love bombing, intermittent reinforcement, devaluation, and jealousy induction. Let's discuss how you can best navigate these tactics during every stage of the trauma-bonding process. As a reminder, the stages of trauma bonding discussed in chapter 3 include love bombing and idealization, cognitive dissonance, intermittent reinforcement, devaluation and identity erosion, and dangerous adaptation and learned helplessness. The narcissist love bombed you to make you dependent on them, created cognitive dissonance by orchestrating betrayals that made you question who they were, then proceeded to use intermittent reinforcement to shift between hot and cold behaviors unpredictably to get you addicted to the abuse cycle. They devalued you and eroded your identity so you became enmeshed with them, and you began to adapt to the abuse cycle as the new normal, resigning to a sense of learned helplessness.

How to Handle Trauma Bond Stages

There are ways to navigate the trauma bond and weaken it no matter what stage of the process you are in or the red flags you may encounter. The following sections will lead you through dismantling toxic manipulation at every stage, using exercises that will engage your rational mind, not your emotional responses. You can also download these exercises at http://www.newharbinger.com/53561.

Stage 1: Love Bombing and Idealization

The love bombing and idealization phase is the phase of the process that is most crucial because it can either begin a life-changing cycle of abuse or disrupt it from continuing. If you can "catch" yourself and navigate these tactics mindfully, you may be able to avoid the toxic cycle altogether.

Be Aware of Red Flags

If you see these red flags, you must make a habit of withdrawing *before* the cycle even has a chance to begin. Detach from any partner who is rushing you instead of allowing the relationship to flow naturally and grow organically.

Watch out for the following:

- Future-faking promises of marriage and children early on in dating

- Asking you to cut off access to resources and independence (e.g., promising to "take care of you" if you quit your job and marry them)

- Manufactured chemistry and similarity (e.g., declaring they are your soulmate; mirroring your interests, goals, and personality)

- Constant contact through phone or excessive dates used to bond you to them early on

You can test a potential dating partner in the following ways:

- **Drop a red herring.** Disclose a minor insecurity or fear (whether real or false) and see if they bring it up in a degrading manner later on.

- **Share your success.** If they try to negate or belittle you or attempt to detract from your success, at the very least, you know they are an envious person and are likely not compatible with you or your goals.

- **Slow down contact.** This doesn't mean necessarily withdrawing interest. When you're busy with a work project or need time to focus on other priorities, how does your dating partner react? In the early stages, a love bomber will grow frustrated that they are not able to control the pace of the relationship and contact you at all times. They will likely sulk, retaliate, or withdraw altogether. This is how you know they are looking more for control than true compatibility.

- **Ask for the bare minimum.** Do this at a time it may pose a slight inconvenience for your dating partner. For example, say you need something from a shop that doesn't deliver, but you're sick and need to stay home. Do they offer to pick it up for you on their way to your house? Or maybe your car isn't working, and you need a short ride somewhere at a time you know they're available at home. Do they offer to give you a lift? An empathic partner will be more than happy to come to the rescue, even if it poses a slight inconvenience for them. A narcissistic or psychopathic partner, not so much.

- **Pay close attention to how a dating partner treats you.** Notice this especially during times you are sick, need a favor, or when you set boundaries. If you tell a dating partner you're not comfortable with premature intimacy, for example, and they still push for sex, or they act indifferent when you're sick, it's clear they don't respect you, your needs, your well-being, or your boundaries.

- **Get to know your dating partner in person.** Rely on in-person dates, instead of constant texting or phone calls, so you can observe their behavior up close and take note of their nonverbal gestures, tone, and facial micro-expressions—subtle cues you can identify if you're trying to understand whether there's a discrepancy between their words and their actions.

How to Handle Love Bombing

As you learned, research indicates that narcissistic individuals tend to demonstrate love-bombing tendencies, and other studies show that these love-bombing tendencies are associated with increased text and media usage (Arabi 2023; Strutzenberg et al. 2016). However, love bombing often ends abruptly as soon as you are sufficiently invested in the relationship.

Regardless of what someone promises you in the future or how much attention they give you in the beginning, do not give "partner" treatment to a person you just began dating. Keep communication at a minimum at the beginning of dating. Resist their attempts to make excessive contact, do not spend your whole day conversing with them, and do not be available whenever they need you. Set a time limit per day of how much time you are willing to spend on any dating partner as you're just beginning to know them, especially through texting. That way, you never get attached to constant contact in the first place. Don't give any person access to your constant whereabouts and activities. They have not earned this level of trust yet. Do not make big or small sacrifices early in dating. For example, do not move in with your dating partner, move across the country, or quit your job if they promise to "take care of you" (rendering you potentially financially dependent and isolated).

By the same token, do not forego your self-care or quality time with friends just to squeeze in a date with this partner. Keep your phone off while you're absorbed in your work, daily activities, hobbies, and interests. Do not make your life one that can be easily infiltrated or taken over by a manipulator who wants to become enmeshed with you. There is a difference between love bombing and a genuine connection that is fostered over time. This means you do not pour a majority of your time, energy, and resources into someone who has not yet proven they are genuinely interested in you long term and has not yet shown you sufficient proof of their good character and integrity. Do not forego your other options, and do not allow this person to consume your mind, thoughts, or future plans. Do not waste your time engaging in attempts to change their behavior; observe their natural behavior and act accordingly based on your boundaries, standards, and needs.

If you're unsure whether a manipulative partner is coming on strongly with love bombing in the beginning, don't match their energy. Rather, sit back and observe. Identify whether this is a short-term manipulation strategy or a signal of genuine excitement about you.

Enforce Boundaries and Standards

You must establish what you won't tolerate by setting boundaries. This means writing down the behaviors and traits you find unacceptable (e.g., I will not allow someone who talks to me in a condescending manner to have access to my life; I will not allow anyone I am seeing to treat me coldly) and acting accordingly to cut ties if a partner shows these red flags—whether it's two, three, or six months down the line. It also means writing down what you do want in a partner (e.g., I want someone who is emotionally validating; my partner should feel happy for my success; my partner and I agree on goals regarding marriage and children).

It's also important to set standards for your dating partners so you can weed out anyone who's not willing to give you the bare minimum effort before dating them—and detach *while* dating them if they're not giving you what you need. For example, perhaps "effort" to you, at least in the short term, looks like being taken out and treated to romantic dates early on in dating, consistent phone calls and texts, and a *healthy* amount of attention and affection (rather than love bombing). Don't feel guilty about setting such standards. See this standard of effort as a form of self-protection against users and manipulators, as many manipulators in the dating world will use low-effort dates to try to date and bed as many people as possible.

These standards will help you select dating partners who are willing to invest their time and resources in you—a potential indicator of interest beyond just a hookup. Even if such a show of romance turns out to be just a manipulation tactic, at least you didn't waste your own resources or too much of your time and energy on a person looking to waste *your* time. This will not weed out all narcissistic people, as narcissists are skilled at romancing their targets, but it will allow you to set a basic standard for how you want to be treated *before* you choose to date them.

This mindset will help you maintain a detached perspective so you don't invest too much in the relationship. When in doubt, "cut it out"— your time, effort, and energy, that is. If you notice your partner pushing your boundaries, big or small, pull back your attention immediately instead of letting them "get away with it just this once." The following exercise will help you define your boundaries and standards.

EXERCISE: Setting Boundaries and Standards for Relationships

Here are some writing prompts you can do in your journal. This exercise is also available at http://www.newharbinger.com/53561.

- Boundaries in a relationship include physical, emotional, spiritual, and financial boundaries. For example, you might have a financial boundary that you will not loan out money to anyone you're dating, or an emotional boundary that you will not tolerate someone speaking down to you. List your physical, emotional, spiritual, and financial boundaries for *new relationships*.

- What boundaries do you feel were crossed in your relationship with a narcissist that you now wish to protect and defend earlier on?

- What preferences do you want in a dating partner (e.g., someone who doesn't drink or smoke; someone who is not in touch with their exes)?

- How will you determine a high-effort partner from a low-effort one? (For example, they plan a date they think you will like rather than inviting you to their place late at night to "watch a movie.")

Stage 2: Cognitive Dissonance

Many survivors struggle with conflicting emotions and thoughts because of the narcissist's false mask and their contradictory actions. Locating beliefs that cause conflicting emotions, rumination, or anxiety can help resolve cognitive dissonance.

EXERCISE: Sort Out Conflicting Thoughts

Here are some writing prompts you can do in your journal or using the worksheet available online.

In your journal, copy the chart below. Then, consider what aspects of your abuser you have a feeling were misrepresented to you based on their long-term behaviors and write these traits and behaviors under "Their Presented Self." Next, think about what their behaviors revealed to you over time. Write these revelations down under "Their True Self." In the middle column "Conflicted," include aspects you weren't sure were part of their presented image or authentic self. Look at the sample chart below for some ideas.

Their Presented Self	Conflicted	Their True Self
They presented themselves as kind, charming, and generous.	There were times they seemed to care about my welfare and health.	They actually punished me for having basic needs in the relationship; they made cruel remarks and didn't take accountability.

- Think about the conflicting behavior or trait carefully. Was it always consistently demonstrated throughout the relationship, or was it inconsistent? How so?

- Were there any contradictory behaviors that didn't align with this conflicting trait? What were they?

- What may have been other motives for demonstrating that behavior other than authentic desire or concern?

Stage 3: Intermittent Reinforcement

As you learned earlier, intermittent reinforcement is when the manipulator blows hot and cold to make you work harder to win their approval and keep you trauma bonded to the relationship. To navigate intermittent reinforcement, "match" the energy and investment of the narcissist so you can withdraw some energy from this connection and use it for your own self-care and goals. Withdraw as soon as you see the narcissist becoming cold toward you. Mirror their indifference. Do not overcompensate for their absence or withdrawal from the relationship by trying to get the narcissist's attention or attempting to reconnect with them. Don't try to further prove yourself or jump through hoops—mindfully notice when you have the impulse to do so. In order to tackle intermittent reinforcement effectively, and not just pretend you're ignoring them but still waiting by the phone, try some of these strategies.

- **Have a self-care activity ready to engage in.** When the narcissist stops texting or calling you as often, start immersing yourself in a self-care activity such as yoga or meditation.

- **Fill your time with something you enjoy.** If the narcissist is giving you the silent treatment, work on a goal or hobby you've been neglecting.

- **Replace unhealthy addictive habits with healthier ones.**
  For example, if you have a habit of constantly chasing after
  the narcissist when they ignore you, physically chase a "runner's high" by taking a jog around the neighborhood instead.
  Or if you find yourself stress eating after arguments with the
  narcissist, drink more water, keep yourself nourished with
  healthy snacks, and surround yourself with healthy distractions and pleasurable activities instead.

EXERCISE: Track Betrayals and Destructive Cycles

It can be hard to see the pattern of intermittent reinforcement when you're
inside a toxic relationship. Keeping track of betrayals and other destructive
cycles, and the love bombing that follows, can help illuminate this cycle.
Here are some writing prompts you can do in your journal or using the
worksheet available online.

- Track when the first betrayal or micro-betrayal happened.
  Then, write down incidents where you noticed the first escalation—something that pushed your boundary beyond how it
  would usually be pushed. How did the narcissist pull you back
  into the relationship after the betrayal happened?

- Track other destructive cycles in your relationship. What
  happens before and after love bombing, for example? How
  long do silent treatments tend to last? Is there usually a sign
  when the toxic person is about to emotionally withhold from
  you? How did they pull you back into the relationship
  afterward?

- Create a timeline to better see how these trauma bonds have
  become strengthened over time. What patterns do you see?

Stage 4: Devaluation and Identity Erosion

In the devaluation and identity erosion stage of the trauma-bonding process, the manipulator begins to demean and belittle you. They can't keep the false mask on for too long because their core lack of empathy will inevitably seep through the cracks. In chapter 3, you learned about the various manipulation tactics narcissists use to keep you trauma bonded to them, including stonewalling, jealousy induction, gaslighting, projection, and distortion. Let's look at how you can navigate these toxic manipulation tactics.

Defeat Stonewalling

If the narcissist stonewalls you during an argument and refuses to discuss problems, use that time period for self-care and pursuing hobbies, interests, and goals that benefit you. Also work on "reality checking." Do a cost-benefit analysis and reframe the relationship using the following exercises. When you look at a toxic relationship through a cost-benefit lens, you are able to see more clearly that it's harming rather than benefiting you.

EXERCISE: Cost-Benefit Analysis of Relationships

Here are some writing prompts you can do in your journal or using the worksheet available online.

- What are the costs of being in a relationship, especially a toxic one? What costs do you incur to your physical health, mental health, energy, goals, self-esteem, resources, and ability to take care of yourself?

- What do you lose when you're in a relationship that's not right for you? What have you lost in the past?

- What are the benefits of being single? For example, what activities can you do when you're free from any obligations to another person? What kinds of emotions can you express freely? How much time can you spend focusing on yourself and pursuing your goals?

EXERCISE: Reframe a Toxic Relationship's Benefits

Here are some writing prompts you can do in your journal or using the worksheet available online.

Create a chart in your journal that looks like the one below. In the first column, list all the perceived benefits you get from the relationship. In the second column, brainstorm alternative ways you can gain that benefit rather than relying on an abusive partner. Look at the sample chart below for some ideas.

Perceived Benefits	Alternative Ways to Receive Benefits
Financial security	I can pursue new career or financial opportunities to make myself more financially stable.

Conquer Jealousy Induction

We've talked about how grandiose narcissists (who are entitled, seek admiration, and believe they are superior) provoke jealousy in their partners for the purposes of gaining power and control, while more vulnerable narcissists (who are more hypersensitive and anxious) induce jealousy to *also* exact revenge on the partner, test and strengthen the relationship, seek security, and compensate for low self-esteem. You may find yourself especially susceptible to being manipulated by jealousy induction. That is why it's so important to develop a strong self-concept of knowing your worth and irreplaceability, so you do not fall into the trap of vying for a narcissist's attention. You must always choose yourself.

Use the exercises in chapter 4 to get in touch with what you love and appreciate about yourself and your life—the unique positive traits and qualities that you have that cannot be replicated in another person. This will help you remember your worth, especially when a toxic person is doing something that goes against the standards that you have for your dating partners.

Here's what you can do to deflect their efforts to make you jealous:

Cultivate irreplaceability and connect with your uniqueness. Make a "love" list for yourself, taking inventory of all the positive qualities others notice in you and that you admire about yourself, as well as your achievements. These qualities can be both external and internal and can include traits that the narcissist may have criticized to deflate your confidence. What successes did they downplay? Look at them with fresh eyes.

Replace unwanted comparisons with acknowledgment of your strengths. There is only one "you" in this world. You bring a unique and special package. The narcissist had to mirror you in order to get you to fall in love with them. Essentially, you fell in love with parts of yourself. It's time to honor your strengths and forego comparisons. What do you have that other people don't? What is the source of your irreplaceable, distinctive "spark"? When you find yourself comparing or ruminating, replace that comparison with a unique or admirable quality you possess.

Make it a habit to compliment yourself. You can do "mirror work" by looking into the mirror and telling yourself loving, soothing affirmations. "I love myself" is a good affirmation to start with. Others might include "I am beautiful in every way" or "I take care of myself." Remember, self-love is not narcissistic. Don't be afraid to heap on some healthy praise.

Overcome Gaslighting

In a relationship with a narcissist or psychopath, your reality and sense of self can feel distorted. They have projected onto you their own flaws and shortcomings and made you believe your strengths are your weaknesses. When you protest, they use gaslighting to make you think it's your fault or you didn't hear what you heard. It's time to take back control over your self-perception and reality.

First, document incidents of gaslighting, preferably with the help of a professional. Write down what the abuser distorted about an incident, followed by the incidents of abuse as they exactly occurred, to identify the discrepancies. Write down what you were feeling before and after the incident as well as any thoughts of confusion (e.g., "Tom called me a terrible name today and told me he was just joking. But he makes these cruel 'jokes' a lot and it's unacceptable"). This "reality checking" can help ground you back into what really occurred and how it affected you. Tap into the more "rational" part of the brain so you don't perceive reality through the emotions the narcissist provoked in you.

As you sift through these incidents of gaslighting, you'll start to notice how the narcissist has caused you to replace the truth with their twisted version of reality. By not allowing them to rewrite history, you hold on to the truth and get closer to breaking the trauma bond.

Vanquish Projection

When looking at how the narcissist engages in projection, write down "translations" of what their behavior and words *really* mean. If the narcissist insults your intelligence even though you naturally outsmart them, write down how they're trying to deflate your confidence because they feel threatened by you. If they claim you are bitter or angry, write down a translation that reveals how the narcissist wants you to forget their abusive actions quickly just so they can escape accountability. For example, you might write down, "Miranda told me that my degrees are useless." Next, your translation could be, "She is envious of my education and my achievements, which surpass hers. She is trying to belittle me to regain control." You can also try writing in the narcissist's own voice: "I am jealous of your achievements and education, which surpass mine. I want to belittle you because it threatens me that you are more educated and successful than I am."

The key here is to help you stop internalizing what the narcissist is explicitly saying and recognize how it distorts reality to benefit them, while disempowering you. Recognize that whatever the narcissist is accusing you of is usually a trait or behavior that better describes them. This will gradually counter the skewed self-perception that keeps you hooked to their validation and approval.

Stage 5: Dangerous Adaptation and Learned Helplessness

To counteract this stage, where the narcissist has made you adapt to their manipulation and you feel helpless to leave the relationship, you need to start building back your self-esteem. Revisit the exercises in chapter 4 to build a strong sense of self.

If you want to give yourself the best chance of healthy self-love and healthy relationships in the future, spend this time processing your traumas and insecurities as much as possible, using the healing modalities discussed in chapter 4. Anyone can be traumatized by a narcissist, but people with childhood trauma or trauma from previous relationships may find themselves having an extra layer of difficulty in cutting ties with narcissistic individuals. That is because the "sweet and mean" cycle of abuse can feel all too familiar and addictive to the brain, especially if you've experienced it before at a vulnerable stage of development.

Working on your insecurities and processing your traumas, preferably with a trauma-informed mental health professional, can help you to detach from narcissistic people with more fervor in the future. You'll be able to identify what wounds and triggers they may have deliberately targeted to exploit you. Once you've worked substantially on your healing, you will have a much better chance of exiting the relationship rather than staying within it just because you've been conditioned to seek a narcissist's comfort after they trigger you. You will rely instead on your healthy coping skills and ability to process your trauma, instead of avoiding the trauma they put you through or rationalizing it as a survival mechanism.

In addition, take charge of your finances, career, and living situation to ensure that you do not become overly dependent on a relationship to validate you. Some people who find themselves having an intense longing and desire for romantic partnership may be subconsciously avoiding the work that is needed in other areas of their lives and unknowingly looking for someone to save them. This can create a void that narcissistic partners can pretend to cater to in the beginning in order to get you to see them as your "savior." Unfortunately, this can escalate into narcissists isolating you and demanding control over you in return. If you find that other areas of your life could benefit from your attention, such as your finances, career goals, living situation, physical health, and friendships, now is the perfect time to work on these areas so you don't fall into this trap of becoming dependent on anyone for validation.

Finally, set a time limit for any continued contact with a narcissist. If you are still struggling and feel unable to go "cold turkey" right away or have circumstances that prevent you from doing so, at the very least set a limit for how much time you will spend interacting with and ruminating over them. By withdrawing your time and energy and redirecting your focus to self-care, priorities, and goals, you train your brain to take the excessive fixation off the narcissist, allowing it to slowly "detox" from the chaotic relationship. The following exercise will help you look forward to a bright future, one without your abuser.

EXERCISE: Skyrocket Your Success

Here are some writing prompts you can do in your journal or using the worksheet available online.

- As you start to detach from the narcissist, get to know yourself and your aspirations for your best life going forward. What would your dream life look like regardless of whether or not you're in a relationship?

- What is the kind of career you'd like to have, or if you already have an established career, what goals are you working on to improve that aspect of your life?

- What would your dream living situation look like and what small steps would you have to take *now* to begin working toward that dream? What larger steps might you take after you're further along in your healing journey?

- Are your current friendships, communities, and support networks nourishing, or do they need a reevaluation? What would these ideally look like?

Dating Red Flags to Watch Out For

In dating narcissists or otherwise toxic people, it's important to familiarize yourself with the red flags of manipulation in its early stages. In addition to the red flags noted earlier in this chapter, look out for the following traits and behaviors of narcissists and psychopaths.

Negging

When narcissistic dating partners feel you are too out of their league or want to make you more susceptible to their romantic advances, they use a manipulation method known as *negging* (or *covert, underhanded attempts to belittle you*). This is not just a narcissistic manipulation tactic— it's also a common method of pick-up artists. Negging can come in the form of playful teasing, but usually it's often weaponized in far more sinister and brutal ways in the dating world. While negging won't work on everyone, research does indicate that lowering someone's self-esteem can make them more compliant with your requests and more open to romantic advances.

Let's say your date remarks, "That dress is quite brave" or "You're a doctor? Do they just let anyone into medical school these days?" These remarks are geared to undermine you, so you feel motivated to prove yourself or win your dating partner over. If you are being negged or feel on edge around a dating partner, it's important to detach. This is not someone with the maturity or willingness to connect authentically with you.

Staged Breakups, the "Dread Game," and Love Triangles

In the pick-up artist's and narcissist's playbook, devaluation is used to instill a perpetual fear of abandonment and anxiety about the fate of the relationship. Narcissists prey on your fear of abandonment by staging breakups (knowing very well they don't actually intend to break up with you), taking sudden "breaks" from the relationship, or evoking jealousy, so that you are more likely to comply with their demands out of the fear of losing them.

They try to "demonstrate value" by pretending they are willing to walk away at any time, even if they have no intention of leaving and are just manipulating you to feel that way. They may even claim, "If you're unhappy, you can leave at any time," when you bring up concerns, even though what they really intend to do is spark your fear of abandonment and ensure you never dare hold them accountable again.

In the "dread game," both narcissists and pick-up artists deliberately try to provoke insecurities and jealousy in you by emotionally withholding throughout the cycle of manipulation. They might subject you to the silent treatment, flaunt other romantic prospects, or become ambiguous and express uncertainty about their commitment to you. This is all deliberate to make themselves seem more valuable or desirable. By putting you in a perceived competition for their attention or affection, they can manipulate dating partners who may not give them attention otherwise. That way, no matter how amazing you are or how amazing the relationship seemed at the beginning, you feel chronically off-kilter and ready to bend over backward trying to please them.

Premature Intimacy

Narcissistic people manufacture a deep connection with you by disclosing personal details about themselves to get you to disclose your insecurities to them, creating a false sense of intimacy that makes you more susceptible to being seduced. They also push for premature physical and psychological intimacy.

Arthur Aron and his fellow researchers (1997) discovered that intimacy between two strangers was strengthened by having them ask each other a series of personal questions. As they note, "One key pattern associated with the development of a close relationship among peers is sustained, escalating, reciprocal, personal self-disclosure." If you encounter a dating partner who asks you intrusive questions, tries to prolong dates, or pretends the connection between you is a lot more advanced than it actually is in the early stages, be wary. For example, if a dating partner asks you invasive questions about your childhood or tells you they want to get married on the first date, that's a red flag.

An empathic person who authentically wants to get to know you will not try to become attached to you in such a fast-paced manner unless there's a hidden agenda. Resist disclosing personal details when a date reveals intimate information so prematurely.

Lack of Relational and Emotional Permanence in Relationships

Have you ever noticed that with a narcissistic dating partner, they tend to devalue you at the drop of a hat, even after a heavy period of love bombing? Psychologists note that narcissistic and psychopathic individuals lack the willingness or ability to maintain a consistent perception of people, including when their partners challenge them, hold them accountable, or harm their ego. This is also known as a lack of relational object constancy and emotional permanence. The narcissist, when they are met with healthy feedback, does not allow themselves to experience both states of "I love and care for this person" and "They hurt my ego or are no longer catering to my needs—how dare they?" simultaneously.

To take it further, I would say they also lack empathy and have an excessive sense of entitlement, and that these are the driving forces behind their harmful and aggressive behaviors. "Out of sight, out of mind" applies to them emotionally because if their ego is harmed or their sense of entitlement rattled, they begin to devalue the very partners they once love bombed without much empathy or remorse, not caring how building a close relationship with someone and then suddenly pretending that person doesn't exist may affect the other person. They may have been pursuing you heavily with supportive calls and texts for months, and suddenly one day, seem annoyed you're even contacting them at all—and there doesn't seem to be any rational explanation for this. Psychopaths demonstrate this on an even more extreme level, as they are prone to boredom and sensation-seeking; as a result, they become easily irritated and bored with the people they may have spent months or years building close bonds and relationships with.

Their lack of emotional depth and range means that while these bonds may look and feel very close and intense, especially to the individual being love bombed, and even feel euphoric and exciting to the psychopath at the time, psychopaths can still grow bored of them, no matter how exciting or wonderful their partners are or how much ecstasy the psychopath derives from love bombing people. To the psychopathic individual, such bonds are merely alliances that can be devalued or discarded at a moment's notice when the target does something to challenge their sense of superiority. Even as both narcissists and psychopaths enjoy the euphoria of love bombing their targets, they are often in search of novelty, even when they are in loving relationships with incredible people.

The partners they love bombed often say, "I don't know how this happened. They were so devoted to the relationship and to me one minute. Then suddenly they're running off with their coworker or comparing me to their new friend in a way that seems to suggest that friend possesses all the qualities they once praised me for." It can feel like the narcissist or psychopath no longer "sees" them or they cease to exist—until, of course, they come back around to extract more resources and energy. The abuser will often do this when they feel they've lost control of the partner or the partner attempts to move forward. This "reignites" the spark in a psychopath's eyes because the partner who becomes tired of the psycho-path's antics tends to intrigue them and offers another form of novelty. However, this only begins the treacherous abuse cycle once more, cement-ing preexisting trauma bonds.

Detoxing from Abuse Cycles and Healing Yourself

On the journey to healing from the narcissist, you may feel tempted to bandage your emotional wounds by jumping into another relationship or pursuing another romance. This is especially tempting if you see the nar-cissist pursuing another target quickly after your own relationship with them. It's important that during the time you heal from the trauma bond and the relationship, you start making peace with being on your own rather than going overboard attempting to rebound with other people. If you are someone who has the habit of avoiding singlehood, now is the perfect time to detox from such harmful cycles of dating.

You may have been conditioned by society to believe that a relation-ship is the only way you can be happy. This may be especially true if you are a woman reading this book, as women tend to be socialized to be caretakers and are taught to depend on relationships or their marital status to derive a sense of self-worth. They are more likely to be shamed for being single. The social pressures of getting into relationships or dating ardently in search of "the one" can cause many people to avoid the healing process and start to look for a partner before they gain discernment of the red flags or do the inner work necessary to ensure they don't stay tethered to a toxic relationship.

It's a myth that a period of singlehood, or even long-lasting single-hood, cannot bring joy and fulfillment. This myth has been *heavily* pro-moted to women. Yet according to Harvard-trained psychologist Dr. Bella DePaulo (2023), who reviewed a wealth of research in the field of relation-ships, studies indicate that single people, including single women, can be just as happy and satisfied with their lives as their coupled counterparts—in some cases, even happier, healthier, and wealthier, with stronger social connections. For example, researchers Böger and Huxhold (2020) compared the satisfaction of 6,188 people who were either single or in a relationship at two points during a six-year time span. For single people, the researchers inquired whether they were satisfied with their singlehood; for partnered people, they asked if they were satisfied with their partnership. The single people in this study indicated they were happy with their singlehood and their satisfaction actually *increased* over six years. Interestingly, for the couples in the study, satisfaction did not reliably increase, and whether or not a person was in a relationship was not necessarily relevant to whether they felt lonely.

This is consistent with other longitudinal research on marriage itself, where a considerable yet temporary "honeymoon effect" is noted. Luhmann and colleagues (2012) analyzed studies totaling 65,911 people and discovered that life satisfaction *decreased* over the months following marriage. Kalmijn (2017) also noted this honeymoon effect in a study of 11,429 adults, which showed an increase in depressive feelings and a decrease in life satisfaction as the marriage continued, with a surprisingly *negative* effect on health. In addition, the study revealed that women specifically tended to experience a *less* negative effect from divorce on their life satisfaction than men did, suggesting that women may fare better in their well-being when they do exit a marriage, perhaps due to the higher level of emotional and domestic labor women are generally expected to undertake in marriage. Another longitudinal study of 12,373 adults did not find that married people became healthier after getting married unless they were in very long marriages surpassing ten years (Tumin & Zheng 2018).

In summary, marriage likely won't save you or your relationship if you aren't already happy and healthy to begin with—whether with your partner or from within. It's not finding a relationship itself that brings us happiness; it really is about finding happiness and satisfaction within, with or without a partner.

Decentering Relationships and Recentering Yourself

If you've been socially conditioned all your life to believe that only romantic relationships can make you happy, the idea of "decentering" relationships from your life and enjoying the peace of singlehood may seem like counterintuitive dating advice. However, it's actually one of the most powerful pieces of advice you can heed if you want to avoid the danger of settling for a toxic or narcissistic person just for the sake of settling down.

As you decenter coupledom from your life, you will also be able to focus on creating a fulfilling, joyful life with plenty of ambitions, hobbies, interests, friendships, and exciting career opportunities. You will build a life that only a truly worthy partner would be able to enter in order to add value to your life. This will make it that much more difficult for narcissists to enter your life or stay, because you will recognize how much they are detracting from the peaceful baseline you've set for your life.

Takeaways

You have now learned how to tackle manipulation at every stage of the trauma bond cycle, enforce healthy boundaries, and detect red flags in dating. You are more equipped with tools to decenter toxic people from your life and reconnect with a stronger sense of self-love and motivation toward your goals moving forward. In the next chapter, we will explore how to maintain sustainable healing as you go "no" or "low contact" with your narcissistic or psychopathic partner.

CHAPTER 6

Breaking Up with Narcissists and Trauma Bonds for Good

One of the most challenging aspects of breaking trauma bonds is literally breaking the bond through a breakup, and one of the most dangerous times for a survivor of abuse is when they are about to leave the relationship. How do you extricate yourself safely from a narcissist, even if you've done the hard work to detach from them? It may seem simple to tell you to "just leave," but clearly, there can be many barriers that prevent you from leaving a relationship safely. Some survivors have to prepare and plan well ahead of time in order to cut ties, and some may be forced to stay longer in the relationship due to their specific circumstances. If you believe you are in any danger from a toxic partner, I urge you to seek help from law enforcement and a therapist and make a safety plan to ensure that you protect yourself from further retaliation or manipulation.

Barriers to Leaving the Narcissist

Use a journal with a lock feature or a secure password-protected notes app to write down the current barriers that you face as you try to leave the narcissist. Brainstorm potential options for countering these barriers. Examples are provided below to help guide you.

Financial Barriers

These may include being financially dependent on the narcissist, being prevented from getting a job or pursuing your education, or being financially abused by the narcissist, who exploits your hard-earned funds for their own gain. You might plan to navigate these barriers by hiring a divorce financial planner, saving up cash secretly, opening a separate bank account and having statements sent to a private email address, or planning to secure temporary shelter prior to getting a job (whether it's going to an actual shelter or living with a friend or family member until you can secure housing).

Children, Legal, and Property Barriers

Perhaps you have children with the narcissist, have pets, or share property with them. I hear from many survivors who are struggling not only with the effects of manipulation in the relationship but also with retraumatization during divorce proceedings, custody hearings, and co-parenting arrangements. These cases often include a narcissistic or otherwise high-conflict personality gaslighting others and using the legal system to further abuse you. To avoid custody battles or losing pets or property, you may feel trapped into staying with the narcissist because you're not sure how you may navigate these issues effectively.

There are steps you can take to facilitate the process of divorce, even when you have children and even with a high-conflict partner. These include equipping yourself with as much information as possible about the local laws in your state regarding property division, spousal support, and child and custody support; speaking with a lawyer who is experienced in dealing with high-conflict personalities; keeping careful documentation of all relevant communication and abuse incidents; petitioning the court for an emergency restraining order if abuse against the children is a factor and ensuring they enforce heavy consequences if such court orders are violated; and maintaining strict boundaries while co-parenting. We'll speak more about the importance of documentation in the section "Insights from Divorce Lawyers."

Emotional and Psychological Barriers

As we've explored throughout this book, there are myriad obstacles that can prevent survivors from leaving the relationship—that is why breaking the trauma bond using the exercises earlier in this book can be so crucial to the process of leaving because it allows you to regain emotional balance and control. Let the stories of other survivors and your enhanced knowledge about the tactics and personality traits of abusers guide you in knowing the abuse was never your fault and that you do not deserve this mistreatment. You deserve freedom and healing.

Cultural Barriers

Not all cultures, religions, faiths, or spiritualities support the idea of divorce. This can create a sense of fear, obligation, and guilt from your communities, especially if you fear the stigma and shame of being divorced. Working through these fears and stigmas with a trauma-informed professional who is familiar with your culture and culturally sensitive can help you better understand how to tackle these barriers while still keeping yourself safe. Sometimes, survivors have to separate themselves from communities that harm them, even though this can be an incredibly painful process.

Insights from Divorce Lawyers

Throughout my career as both a journalist and a researcher, I have interviewed multiple lawyers who were experienced in custody issues and co-parenting. You can find some of the original interviews by searching for my article, "Divorcing and Co-Parenting with Narcissists: Divorce Lawyers Share Tips for Handling High Conflict Personalities in Court." Below I provide a summary and analysis of some of the most important insights gained from these interviews.

Keep Documentation

Keep a detailed record and documentation of what occurred in the relationship. Whether it's video, audio recordings (provided that these are legal in your state), or screenshots of texts and emails, these can all help build your case in a legal battle with a narcissist and speak to their lack of parental competence, parental neglect, or a threat of parental harm to children when negotiating custody. Document all cases of behavior that has harmed the children. Keep discussions centered on the needs of the children when co-parenting.

Stick to written channels of communication that can be easily documented during divorce or custody proceedings or co-parenting situations. Avoid unnecessary and excessive contact beyond the custody agreement and divorce settlement. Keep communication factual and direct, avoiding asking questions that might invite the narcissist to provide unsolicited feedback.

Use apps such as Our Family Wizard or 2Houses to communicate and keep track of what is being said, and keep communication restricted to the app whenever possible. These apps are helpful for sharing calendars, reimbursement transactions and requests, and important documents, and they often record dates and time stamps to streamline the process.

Make a Parenting Plan

If you both share custody, create and stick to a detailed parenting plan that precisely outlines each parent's visitation schedules and responsibilities, as well as any restrictions on communication between you two. Document when the narcissistic parent has failed to meet the responsibilities outlined in that plan.

How to Navigate Custody Hearings and Divorce Proceedings

Custody hearings and divorce proceedings tend to be emotionally charged. Both inside and outside of court, stick to the facts. Avoid giving narcissistic individuals emotional responses to their provocative questions or claims. Whenever possible, get familiar with your own trigger points so you know when the narcissist is trying to deliberately provoke you. Take an inventory of the actions and words from the narcissist you feel tend to trigger you; ground yourself before any interactions, using breathing techniques, and have potential responses ready and prepared to anticipate their false claims. In court, you must remain nonreactive and stick to the facts, as the narcissist will attempt to paint you as irrational. Any time they try to gaslight you, unsettle you, or belittle you in legal proceedings, exercise the "broken record" method by continually stating the facts and referring to the corresponding documentation as evidence.

Other techniques are the BIFF method (keeping your requests brief, informative, friendly, firm), the Gray Rock method (created by the writer and survivor known as Skylar), and the Reverse DARVO method. In the Gray Rock method, you essentially become a gray rock—boring, neutral, and resistant to provocation or manipulation. As the narcissist attempts to get a reaction from you, you give them nothing. In the Reverse DARVO method, you **d**etach yourself from the "story" and emotions of the situation and ground yourself. You then **a**ssert yourself confidently without being aggressive (preferably through written, documented communication) and make a specific **r**equest to meet your needs. Next, you **v**alidate your own emotions and honor your own perspective regardless of any gaslighting you're experiencing, and carefully **o**bserve the reactions of the person to see if they are willing to cooperate or if you need to try a different strategy. With narcissistic people, they will likely not try to de-escalate the situation. But this method can be useful in knowing how to assert yourself and honor your own needs.

Some survivors may benefit from a more collaborative legal process where lawyers bring in other consulting experts, such as therapists, psychologists, or financial experts. It depends on your specific situation, as the narcissist may be able to use these experts against you depending on the resources they have. However, in some cases, it may work in your favor to provide a more detailed presentation of the evidence.

The narcissist may attempt to provoke you and upstage you outside of court during the divorce proceedings or custody negotiations, flaunting their new partner in your face or trying to pit your children against you so they can push you over the edge. Again, continue to stick to the facts and be as mindfully nonreactive as you possibly can. It is important not to compete with a narcissist, even when they try to make everything a competition. Calling them out or trying to convince them of your worth will only keep you more stuck in the trauma bond. Engaging with a narcissist is a unique "game" in that you win more when you're not even playing at all. When you do have to play, reduce their significance and impact. Their frantic attempts to deflate your joy and compete with you is a sign they are losing control and trying to reestablish a false sense of superiority because they don't want to be discarded by you. See these attempts for what they are: manipulation designed to keep you in the toxic cycle.

Avoid Couples Therapy

If you are not yet in divorce proceedings from the narcissist, avoid couples therapy, as many couples therapists will further invalidate the abuse occurring and focus on the toxic dynamics of the relationship as a problem stemming from both of you rather than identifying the abuse. This may prolong the relationship and further gaslight you into feeling like you're the problem when you try to leave. Instead, seek individual therapy with a trauma-informed professional who is well-versed in narcissistic personalities and the dynamics of domestic abuse.

Strategies for Breaking Up with the Narcissist

Leaving a narcissist can be one of the most dangerous times of the abuse cycle. It's no wonder so many survivors attempt to leave several times before they truly leave for good. That is why it's important to work with a therapist, law enforcement, and a lawyer if you are in a difficult situation where you fear retaliation. Below are some strategies you may want to think about if you are preparing to leave. These can all be adapted to your unique circumstances, and when in doubt, always seek help from authorities or support from your therapist if you fear you may be in danger.

Build an Escape Plan Secretly

No matter what strategy you use in breaking free from the narcissist, it's important that you work with law enforcement or a therapist to keep yourself safe. One important safety tip to keep in mind is that telling the narcissist you plan to leave them can place you in danger. They may escalate their abuse, retaliate physically, or attempt to love bomb you into staying, pretending to be the person they were in the beginning of the relationship and dangling the carrot to keep you invested in them.

At times, creating an escape plan requires a level of justified deception to keep yourself safe—what I like to call the "great illusion." For this breakup technique, you temporarily act as if nothing has changed in your relationship with the narcissist, even if you are planning to leave them. You may even pretend that their manipulation methods (such as love bombing) are working and that you are still under their spell. This will help you stay under the radar and flee their detection as you plan your escape safely.

While they assume you're still invested in them and would never leave them, you will use this period of time to strategically prepare: getting your finances together, documenting the abuse if you want to bring a legal case, consulting with a divorce lawyer, researching custody laws in your state, or looking for your new home. This breakup method can be especially effective in cases where you are cohabiting with or are married to the narcissist, or if there is a threat of immediate retaliation or narcissistic rage. If you are escaping a physically violent relationship of any kind, ensure that you already have a safety plan in place.

Do a Slow Fade

This technique is used to detach from the narcissist in a way that is incremental, in small habits that enable you to desensitize yourself slowly to their absence while escaping their notice. If you are not ready to leave the relationship yet or have other barriers in the way of leaving, the slow fade can be a more flexible way to recondition yourself to enjoying life without their interference. This is ideal for situations where you are not living with the narcissist, as some abusers may physically isolate and punish you for daring to live a life outside of them. This is also best for situations where the narcissistic individual is already devaluing you and attempting to use intermittent reinforcement (an alteration of mean and kind behavior) to keep you trauma bonded to them by giving you the bare minimum mixed with random incidents of affection and attention. While you're doing the slow fade, use these tips to keep yourself focused on your goals and "compensate" yourself for the time and energy you spent on the narcissist with nourishing things you do for yourself instead.

- Count the number of incidents of betrayal you experienced. Estimate a number if you need to. You can keep that number or multiply it if you wish. Now, brainstorm the exact number of kind things you can do for yourself. Write them down and do them!

- Decide how you can stay loyal to yourself. You might say, "From now on, I will notice actions and behaviors that make me uncomfortable, and find a way to either get my needs met or enforce boundaries." See chapter 5 for tips and exercises on enforcing boundaries.

- List all the things you can do now that you've detached and cut ties from the narcissist.

- List the things you won't miss experiencing in this relationship with the narcissist.

- Understand that, at times, you will have to "betray" the narcissist in order to avoid betraying yourself. This is to help you cut through the fear, obligation, and guilt you may experience when doing the slow fade. "Betrayal" in a narcissist's eyes can mean anything that questions or threatens their excessive sense of entitlement.

- Look at the agents that strengthen the trauma bond (e.g., continuing physical affection with the narcissist, contacting the narcissist, low self-esteem) versus the ones that weaken it. Ask yourself how you can weaken the agents that fortify the trauma bond and strengthen the support systems that allow you to overcome it. If you're going about your everyday life on autopilot, it's hard to always see the habits that are keeping you attached to the narcissist. For example, you might be going to the grocery store and start habitually thinking about how you're going to cook a lavish meal for the narcissist when you get home. But when you focus on weakening your bonds, it repositions you to consider what healthy foods you would like to pick up instead, returning the focus to yourself instead of people-pleasing. These micro-habits can shape your mindset toward yourself and away from the narcissist.

"Reverse Discard" Combined with the Gray Rock Method

The reverse discard is a method where you subtly persuade the narcissist to discard you first. This can reduce the chances of narcissistic rage or retaliation because they will feel as if the breakup is their own doing and that they "won."

One of the most effective ways to induce a reverse discard is by using what is known as the Gray Rock method mentioned earlier. This is when you become flat, boring, and lifeless to the narcissist in a way that they cannot extract narcissistic supply (e.g., praise, attention, sex, resources, ego strokes, positive or negative reactions) from you anymore. If using the Gray Rock method, keep your interactions with the narcissist as brief and indifferent as possible, embodying nonchalance and neutrality. If the narcissist asks you questions, offer "yes" or "no" replies or responses that exhibit *acknowledgment* but not engagement, like "Hmm," "Interesting," "I see," or "Thanks for telling me that." Narcissists and psychopaths thrive when they're able to create chaos in your life, but once they realize they can no longer provoke the same emotions and reactions as they once did, they become dissatisfied and will seek narcissistic supply elsewhere.

Note: I don't recommend this method if you are not already emotionally detached from the narcissist to a certain extent, as it can create distress at the idea of them moving on to another victim. However, some situations call for the reverse discard to keep yourself safe.

Cold Turkey and the Last Straw Method

Cold turkey endings are best for survivors who are already mentally ready to leave the relationship but need that final "push" to end it with finality. You may or may not need to experience a last straw to finally go cold turkey for good; instead, you might wait for a minor incident that finally shows you the mistreatment in the relationship.

You may be mentally ready to go cold turkey if:

- You feel that the costs and dangers of the relationship outweigh any perceived benefits.

- You find it hard to romanticize the toxic aspects of the relationship anymore, and there is less of a fear of missing out and an escalating sense of danger and urgency to leave as soon as possible to prevent more pain.

- You have given up on trying to "compete" for the narcissist in response to their manufactured love triangles.

- You can see through gaslighting more clearly, and can grapple with the reality in front of you rather than how you wish the circumstances could be.

- You are too emotionally exhausted to try to "make things work" or attempt to "fix" or change the narcissist, or you have radically accepted that this is the narcissist's character and you will likely not be getting back the same person you first met.

- You have built stronger support networks and have a head start on obtaining resources and professional support that can facilitate the process of leaving.

To hold yourself accountable for going cold turkey, you may choose to tell a trusted friend about ending the relationship or do something too "final" to backtrack too easily on (such as signing the lease on a new apartment far away from the narcissist or removing them on all social media channels—any step that reminds you of how far you've come and that will push you to take those final additional steps to leave for good). Cold turkey endings entail cutting all contact with the narcissist and their cronies and removing any reminders of the narcissist from your life. You do not allow the narcissist to ensnare or "Hoover" you back into the cycle of abuse, nor do you give them any opportunity or means to contact you.

Some individuals find it too difficult to leave a narcissist due to deep-rooted abandonment issues and the strength of the trauma bond. That is why they will remain in the relationship until they have had enough. This technique is not recommended for most people due to the risk of trauma, but it will help some people who otherwise might not leave to exit an abusive relationship for good without looking back and make use of their time in the relationship.

Sometimes survivors feel the compulsion to "check" if the narcissist really is as harmful as they think they are due to the heavy amount of cognitive dissonance that has resulted from the relationship. Since they already feel too "stuck" to exit the relationship, they approach this as an exercise to continually experience the truth of the abuser's true self until they have seen what they have needed to see—the extent of the abuser's malice, callousness, and lack of empathy for them. While this is occurring, survivors can use reality checking to identify the tactics they're experiencing and document the abuse with the help of a therapist. Only then do they connect with their authentic outrage at being violated and resolve some of the cognitive dissonance as they see the abuser's true self behind the false mask. This helps them sever the trauma bond as they feel empowered to leave.

The Narcissist's Orchestrated Breakups

As described in chapter 5, there will be situations where you're not the one doing the breaking up—the narcissist may seem to throw you away, or they may orchestrate a "break" to keep you hyperfocused on them while they pursue other targets. If that's the case and you feel a lack of closure, it's important to keep the following reality checks in mind. The narcissist breaks up with people for very different reasons than people usually break up. It's vital you do not blame yourself during this time.

Satisfying Their Need to Win

Narcissists and psychopaths want to gaslight you into believing you were the problem all along and ensure that they're the ones who leave "first" as a power play. This gaslighting tends to be very effective, as narcissists and psychopaths use legitimate-sounding phrases to break up with their partners, such as "This isn't going to work," "I am done," and "I just can't do this anymore," to express their so-called exasperation and disapproval of you during a breakup.

However, while empathic partners may use these phrases to express their valid sense of not being able to be in this kind of relationship anymore, narcissists misuse these phrases to gaslight you after a long period where *they* were the ones mistreating and manipulating *you*, love bombing you intermittently throughout the relationship, and dangling the carrot of false hope that they would change back into the sweet, loving person they portrayed themselves to be at the beginning of the relationship to keep you hooked. They could have faked remorse and begged you for your forgiveness many times to prevent you from leaving them—*this was just a power play so they could leave you first.*

Narcissists and psychopaths feel an intrinsic need to "win" and make you feel like you are the problem rather than them. This is an ego preservation tactic. You would essentially "win" the breakup if you felt validated in the abuse you experienced—this is how a narcissist or psychopath views such an ending because they see relationships not as partnerships but as intricate chess games. They desire to depict you as the main culprit, painting you with unsavory qualities and traits you do not possess.

If you have experienced their chronic manipulation, you need to know that you were not the problem here. When they break up with you, it can feel abrupt, callous, cold, and emotionless. That is because, unbe-knownst to you, narcissists and psychopaths may have been planning the discard for longer than you might expect, plotting strategically to gain ultimate power over you and demean you. There is no better opportunity for a narcissist to try to emotionally debilitate a partner than during a breakup. However, that doesn't mean they won't return—as noted earlier, narcissists can return many times after the ending of the relationship to ensure they still maintain power over you and possibly retain access to resources and sex.

A Ploy to Keep You Fixated on Them

Since they can longer control you, they want to leave you traumatized and hyperfixated on them while they search for new targets they can control. Narcissists and psychopaths enjoy a challenge, and they can target very intelligent, good-looking, successful, empathic, ambitious, and assertive people. They feel fulfilled and powerful knowing they can break down even the strongest of individuals by identifying their vulnerabilities and weaponizing both their strengths and their weaknesses against them.

However, even narcissists and psychopaths have "limits." If they feel they can no longer control you because you see through their false mask, understand their true nature accurately, and are no longer under their spell, they know they will have to put in far more effort, time, energy, and investment to keep you around—something they'd rather avoid doing because they know an easier "shortcut" is to terrorize you enough so you never forget them and inadvertently develop a traumatic bond with them instead.

When you are no longer willing to rationalize their abusive behavior, dismiss the red flags, or minimize their transgressions, narcissists and psy-chopaths know that a breakup will devastate you enough to keep you trauma bonded to them whenever they choose to come back, while at the same time leaving them free to hunt for other more vulnerable targets who are more susceptible to their manipulation and unaware of their true character. This is why you may receive an "I miss you" or "I've been thinking about you" text weeks or months after a breakup. Beware: they don't miss you; they miss controlling you. They are likely looking for an opportunity to keep you thinking about them after the breakup, and some may even try to pit you against another target to make you jealous.

Narcissists are notorious for trying to provoke jealousy long after the relationship has ended, especially through social media. If you do choose to reengage with them, rest assured that they will begin the manipulation all over again, with an even fiercer intensity than the first time around. They enjoy punishing targets over whom they lost control and also enjoy demeaning targets they look at as "gullible" enough to take them back. If you have fallen into this trap, it's important not to blame yourself, as the trauma bond can be both addictive and difficult to extricate yourself from.

Another Way of Demonstrating Power

Narcissists and psychopaths want to maintain significance in your life. Some targets do not fall for their charms as easily as the narcissist would like them to. You may have resisted the narcissist's manipulation by refusing to open up to them, "failing" to disclose your vulnerabilities and traumas, or even identifying their manipulation tactics. Despite this, they still want to establish a sense of importance and significance in your life. They want to feel like *they* are the ones in control.

They inherently know that you will feel overwhelmed by a breakup, so they usually stage or orchestrate the breakup to maintain their significance in your life, even if you were not interested in pursuing anything long term with them, and even if they plan to return. Narcissists associate this kind of "rejection" and loss with need, longing, and desire. That's because when they are rejected themselves, they incur a narcissistic injury and often chase after those who reject *them* in an effort to punish the other person and regain validation. Narcissists thus expect that if *they* break up with someone, others will chase them in turn because that is what they would do in the same situation.

That is why they expect you to pine for them after the breakup and orchestrate the breakup as a way to make themselves memorable to you. It momentarily positions them as "higher" than you as they break the news to you with an air of false superiority and contempt. This is a tactic they use frequently to demean those they perceive to be otherwise out of their league. If you are suffering from a breakup with a narcissist, take heed: it was never about you; it was always about their need for power and control.

How to Reclaim Your Power

To reclaim your power, consider taking the following actions. These are based on the steps and healing modalities you learned earlier, and they will further help you heal from a breakup with a narcissist.

Gamify Your Healing Milestones

One powerful way to get yourself motivated to heal from a breakup with a narcissist is by "gamifying" your goals. In other words, treat it like a game you play tactfully and constructively to benefit yourself. Pair the positive habits you want to reinforce with rewards and pleasure that will motivate you each time you engage in this behavior—this is classical conditioning at its finest. A reward system presents a brilliant framework to "score points," figuratively speaking, every time we use our strengths and abilities to achieve something, no matter how big or small. Clinical trials have shown that rehabilitation programs that "gamify" goals allow people to effectively transition into self-care after traumatic events that have affected their well-being (Worthen-Chaudhari 2021).

You can approach your healing more strategically by setting up smaller goals that you can reach before you achieve the bigger ones. For example, a smaller goal of healing may be developing a routine of going for a fifteen-minute walk in the morning. As you learned in earlier chapters, exercise increases chemicals in the brain that enhance neuron growth—a vital aspect of healing the traumatized brain, where there tends to be neural atrophy. Exercise also releases feel-good neurotransmitters that help you overcome your addiction to the narcissist.

You'll eventually level up to larger goals, but tackle the smaller ones first. To reward yourself for taking on healthier habits, every time you take that morning walk (or yoga session or meditation), reward yourself with something, like a delicious cup of your favorite coffee, an extra snuggle session with your pet, or watching another episode of your favorite television show.

You may find it helpful to share your progress with loved ones, trusted friends, or family members too; research reveals that social reinforcement can boost the effectiveness of our reward system (Jones et al. 2011). You may text a friend a picture from your daily run, or post an encouraging caption on social media noting a milestone you reached. As you get comfortable with achieving smaller stepping-stones, gradually raise the bar by leveling up your goals to bigger milestones: the fifteen-minute walk may become a twenty-minute run, an hour-long hike, or a gym routine. Soon, your healing goals will become an ingrained part of your well-being and self-care regimen.

Replace Self-Sabotaging Behaviors with "Level-Up" Activities

In addition to generating good habits, make sure that you are taking an inventory of the habits that harm you or propel you toward self-sabotage. The narcissist's verbal and psychological abuse has likely trained you to engage in self-sabotage and self-harm, making you internalize false beliefs about your worthiness. As mentioned in chapter 4, you can counter these beliefs through substitute activities that communicate to yourself that you are worthy of being treated better.

Fuel whatever anger you have toward the ways they degraded you into your "glow-up" and "level-up" goals. If you want to kick butt at school or work, now is the perfect time to channel your anger toward the narcissist into productive outlets. If you want a "revenge glow-up," this is the perfect opportunity to sculpt both your brain and your body in ways *you* find most empowering and confidence-inducing for you.

Replace self-sabotage with micro-habits that allow you to flourish. For example, do you find yourself ruminating the first moment you wake up in the morning? Rumination can be a normal part of the healing journey and can signal processing, but incorporating a breathing exercise (such as box breathing, see page 118) when you wake up may help you be more mindful and prepare you for your day so you are less anxious. Set yourself up to win.

Are you checking social media or your phone to see if the narcissist has tried to contact you? Practice putting your phone on airplane mode during times you don't need it and every time you have an urge to do anything related to the narcissist. Instead, use your computer to focus on the work you *do* need to do, or listen to positive affirmations. Install browser extensions like StayFree to prevent social media websites from being accessible—this will enhance your productivity rather than placing your focus elsewhere.

Do you tend to criticize yourself whenever you look in the mirror? Use that opportunity to compliment yourself, provide extra incentive toward any fitness goals you have, or wear your favorite outfit and take a photo to tap into that "glow-up" energy.

Any time you're tempted to romanticize the narcissist in your mind or engage in a harmful, addictive activity to numb your emotions (like drinking, gambling, shopping, or smoking), replace it with an activity that benefits your well-being, health, and fitness. This could be as intensive as going to the gym for a full workout or as low effort as dancing in your room or grabbing a green juice. Over time, replacing your self-sabotaging behaviors with these micro-habits will allow you to flourish long term. It will also communicate to your subconscious that you feel worthy and deserving of self-care rather than punishment.

Refocus on Healing and Turn Your Triggers Into Power

You may have spent excessive time ruminating over the narcissist or constantly visualizing the worst-case scenarios due to the fear of abandonment the narcissist instilled in you. Our brains can be wired toward seeking pleasure or avoiding pain: use this to your advantage when weakening the trauma bond (Stephenson-Jones et al. 2020). If you're in the stage of your healing journey where you feel unmotivated and helpless, visualize that each time you feel joy, it depletes the narcissist of energy and decreases their power, while returning to you all the power they took away. This will motivate you to look for opportunities to achieve your goals and seek out more joy and fulfillment every day. Any time you're triggered, use it as an opportunity to use one of the breathing or mindfulness techniques discussed in this book to regulate your nervous system and then turn your focus toward a desire you want instead. As this becomes a daily habit, it will train your brain toward healing rather than rumination.

Wire your brain toward seeking pleasure rather than avoiding pain, as you have been accustomed to doing in a toxic relationship. When you remember this, it will motivate you to find more opportunities to experience joy—to laugh, connect with others, enjoy nature, take pleasure in your life's joys, be grateful for all the miracles in your life, and kick some extra butt on that goal or project. It will also make you more determined to steer away from self-sabotaging behaviors if you imagine that each time you self-destruct, it only gives the narcissist more power. Visualize this whenever you're tempted to check up on the narcissist on social media or skip your daily self-care routine. It will remind you that the benefit comes from upleveling yourself and not remaining stagnant in the old energy of the toxic relationship and trauma bond.

Go "No Contact" or "Low Contact"

If you do not have children with the narcissist and do not have legal matters to sort out, it's possible to go full "no contact." For those who share children or must maintain contact in some way (for example, in a work setting), it can be a more difficult journey, but it is doable with "low contact."

"No contact" or "low contact" is not just about you reaching out to the narcissistic person; it is also about detaching yourself from triggers related to them and reducing opportunities for them to contact *you.* Mindfully observe your cravings for contact whenever they arise and radically accept that you may have the yearning to reach out or check if they have reached out to you. This is normal. Take time to pause before acting on any cravings. Given that toxic love affects your brain much like cocaine does, going no contact is similar to detoxing from a drug addiction—except, instead of a drug, you're detoxing from another human. For addicts, usually at least ninety days of rehab is needed for this kind of detoxing to have a positive impact, and relapse is often an inevitable part of the journey. For addictions or trauma bonds to toxic relationships, it's possible you may have lapses in judgment, or go back to the relationship—but there will come a time where you will simply be "done" and will want to push forward in your recovery.

For example, if you know that the narcissist tends to contact you through a certain phone number or email address, you may consider getting a new phone number or email address so you can avoid any attempts for them to contact you through this medium. You may avoid places you know they frequent, like certain restaurants or stores, and find alternative arrangements. If you are currently following the narcissistic person on social media, they will likely weaponize this against you by posting pictures or captions that attempt to trigger you.

It's best to take the narcissistic person and any mutual friends off of social media at this time. If you find this too overwhelming to do at any stage, many social media platforms also have the option to simply "hide" them from your newsfeed, or you can take a break from social media yourself by deleting any apps that provide the temptation to check up on them. Sometimes, this can take the edge off your cravings because rather than cutting ties immediately, you give yourself the option of a break from them, which reconditions you to feeling more peaceful about their absence. You essentially "trick" your mind into believing that there is no need for longing or craving because you don't remove the option of contact in a way that makes it even more tempting; you just make the option less available to you.

You may also wish to cut ties with any mutual friends and family members of your toxic ex-partner because they may try to pit these people against you or use them to collect information about you. If you are going "low contact," brainstorm and write down the parameters, boundaries, and limits of this. What does "low contact" mean for you? Perhaps it means that you do not speak to the narcissist about anything except children, property, or businesses you both share, and only talk about legal matters in the presence of your lawyer. Maybe you only use a third-party application, like OurFamilyWizard or the ones described previously, to maintain contact with the narcissist and avoid text messages and phone calls altogether, preventing them from contacting you. You might have an agreement that they are not allowed to show up at your house unannounced and that visitation schedules with the children will be strictly enforced.

If you are maintaining "low contact" with a narcissist outside of a romantic relationship, such as a family member, you may limit the holidays you spend with them, choose not to spend any special occasions with them, or make phone calls or text messages very brief and factual. Work with your lawyer and therapist to customize these suggestions to your particular circumstances.

Reminders for Staying "No Contact"

The following closing reminders can help you stay "no contact" with a narcissist. Refer to this list frequently as you detox from the narcissist or have a craving to reach out to them.

Every time you stay "no contact," you are protecting yourself. You are preventing further psychological violence and harm. Every time you choose not to contact, respond to, check up on, or seek validation from a toxic partner, you communicate to yourself that you value yourself, your time, your new life of freedom, and your human right not to be subjected to further toxicity, abuse, abandonment, or mistreatment. Every time you maintain no contact, you protect yourself from traumatizing information or psychological violence that could retraumatize you and trap you back into an abuse cycle, a cycle that will only subject you to more pain, more heartache, and a pervasive sense of hopelessness. You don't have to let yourself reenter a seemingly inescapable situation again, as it will get harder to leave each time you do.

You deserve to be safe, healthy, and happy. You may feel separate and different from other people because of what you've endured. However, you are just like any other human being—you have the exact same rights and are entitled to the same boundaries as anyone else who has not been in a toxic relationship. There are many people who are in healthy relationships and free from toxicity—and as a human being, you are *so worthy* of the same.

You have an inner strength that is greater than any trauma bond. It may come as a surprise to you, but narcissistic and psychopathic abusers don't actually hold any authentic inner power—they take away power from others because they have none within themselves. They lack a sense of core identity, and often they need you more than you need them (even if it feels otherwise). They leech off of your light—you are *their* life source, their narcissistic supply, and they tend to benefit from your resources, talents, and compassion. Without it, they are lost and chasing yet another vulnerable target to meet their needs. Remember the light, the talents, the gifts, the strengths, and the joy that have always been and still are within you.

Your will is stronger than any toxic person's attempts to bully you. If you're suffering from PTSD or complex PTSD, you may hear your abuser's voice as your own inner critic. You may have been met with attempts to shame or love bomb you back into the abuse cycle. You may be left reeling from the bullying behavior of your ex-partner. You may not understand why your abusive ex-partner refuses to leave you alone, stalks or harasses you, or even goes so far as to flaunt their new partner as a way to taunt and provoke you. These can be incredibly painful experiences, but as you heal and process these traumas, you will learn to prioritize your freedom over their attempts to bully you. The bullying may hurt and you will have to address it as you process the trauma, preferably with a professional, but where there is a strong will, there is an even stronger survivor who can meet any challenge along the way.

Their lies will never replace your truth. You may experience the overwhelming ordeal of a narcissistic abuser attempting to smear and slander you, or even threaten to release personal information about you, especially if you have "discarded" them first. Their narcissistic rage and injury propels them to regain power by putting you through an even worse "discard" to essentially "win" the breakup or save face. Although some of these are empty threats meant to destabilize you, more malignant narcissists may follow through with their threats. However, you do have a degree of agency in how you respond to their threats. You have options to protect yourself, so document those threats in case you need to ever take legal action. You can go to law enforcement if you have to (and feel safe doing so). You can also seek support from a lawyer and counselor who can offer you insights into your particular situation. What you *don't* have to do is immediately give in to the threats of emotional blackmail and go back into an abusive relationship only to be terrorized in an even worse fashion than before. Even in the toughest situations, make a note of all your options and choices.

You're allowed to protect and defend yourself, no matter what. Whether that means getting a restraining order, changing your number, or blocking them on all social media platforms, do whatever you need to do to protect yourself from the narcissist's manipulation and abuse. You don't deserve to be retraumatized in any way, shape, or form. Seek support from your local domestic violence shelter, find a trauma-informed therapist, research local support groups, or try group therapy focused on trauma recovery and support. Find any and all support you can to help build and reinforce the fortress of protection around you. The more high-quality resources and support you have, the more confident and at ease you'll be in moving forward without your toxic ex-partner.

Show compassion for yourself, and keep going. No matter how difficult it becomes, be gentle with yourself and never give up. Even if you make a mistake or give in to an urge to contact the narcissist, all is not lost. That is how you truly overcome an addiction; you don't let imperfection hinder you from progressing on your path. You keep going. If you fell off the wagon and broke "no contact" (whether by checking up on the narcissist or responding to them), don't judge yourself too harshly. Self-judgment leads to the same sense of unworthiness that makes you look for validation from toxic people. *Instead, get back on the wagon and commit yourself to the journey even more fully.* Use this as a learning module for the real "test."

Practice mindfulness and radical acceptance of any urges you might have without acting on them and participating in more self-sabotage. Know that every setback is simply bringing up the core wounds you need to heal in order to move forward with even more determination than before. Identify the triggers that led to your decision to break "no contact" to prevent them in the future. Shatter the "false mask" the narcissist presented; it never truly existed. The promise of a relationship that was fabricated in the love-bombing phase led you to an investment that ultimately entailed more loss than gain.

Your life is worth more than empty promises. If a narcissist or psychopathic individual is reaching out to you to reconnect and make the same promises they made in the beginning of the relationship, swearing to change, love, and care for you, yet they invalidated, belittled, and degraded you throughout the relationship, please be wary. These are empty promises orchestrated to control and coerce you back into the abuse cycle. Don't feed into the illusion of what the relationship could have been. Instead, acknowledge it for what it was: a cycle of terror that included false promises that were never carried out. You deserve healthy love and self-love. The true promise of a new and healthier life awaits you: make a promise to yourself that you will create that joyful new reality instead.

You are strong and resilient enough to heal from the trauma. But you don't have to be strong and resilient enough to endure more of it. You've likely developed a high level of resilience and a pain threshold that could rival a sumo wrestler's. You may feel like you're capable of coping with more of the narcissist's tactics, but remember that this is truly a life-or-death situation. Some narcissistic and psychopathic individuals are physically violent and in extreme cases have murdered their partners.

Emotional abuse is also violence. You might not think of emotional violence as a life-or-death situation, but considering the suicides that occur as a result of bullying and the fact that domestic violence survivors are at a higher risk of committing suicide, it's truer than you might think (McManus et al. 2022).

Each time you sacrifice your peace of mind to pursue or chase the abuser, rather than detoxing from the relationship, you reenact that same sense of hopelessness and powerlessness you experienced during the abusive relationship. This can pose severe harm to your psyche over time due to the cumulative impact of traumatic and retraumatizing experiences. By breaking "no contact," you convince yourself that you are unworthy of something more. In the case of life or death, always choose a new life without your abuser and the trauma bond.

Balance mixed emotions with reality checks. Mixed emotions about your toxic ex-partner are normal, but it's important to take off the rose-colored glasses and replace your longing with reality checks. You may find yourself romanticizing about your ex-partner, especially in times of turmoil, distress, life adversity, or loneliness. You may even wonder whether it was worth leaving the toxic relationship during these times. You may experience mixed emotions about your abuser as the "good times" come flooding back.

Remember: you were the only one truly invested in the good times. For your abuser, those good times were simply a form of periodic love bombing, a form of intermittent reinforcement that kept you under their control while feeding you crumbs or dangling the carrot of a future they did not intend to carry out. The good memories you had with the narcissist never justify the emotional abuse they subjected you to.

Acknowledge and honor your loneliness, but know that it too will pass. It can actually be a sign that you are working through, actively healing, and processing the traumas you've experienced. It's a signal that you may need to be more present with yourself, enjoy your own company more, and surround yourself with better support networks. Acknowledge and validate the loneliness, but don't resist it by pursuing more toxic people or going back to the same toxic relationship. You may need a period of hibernation to reflect and recover from the trauma before you date or pursue new friendships. Take this time to heal and don't rush the process: it's very much needed in order for you to be in an optimal state of mental health. While you don't want to self-isolate completely (having a professional in your corner can help), it's necessary to reserve your energy for your own healing at this time. The more healed you are, the less likely you will settle for toxic relationships and friendships in the future.

You are not an emotional punching bag for the abuser. Relationships with narcissistic people are not healthy and reciprocal. Instead, you are used as an emotional punching bag. They take their flaws, insecurities, and projections and spew these onto you. You have been trained by your abuser to tolerate this as a natural part of the relationship. No more. You deserve more than to be someone's emotional punching bag. You deserve a mutually respectful relationship where love and compassion are the default.

It's up to you to make sure an emotional vampire doesn't become nourished on your supply while you're left drained and malnourished after an interaction with them. Without their source of supply, narcissists live in the darkness of their own emotional void. Don't let your mind, your body, and your soul be part of their feeding queue. Remove yourself completely from the equation. When they don't get to feast upon your emotions, your commitment, and your investment, you get to nourish yourself with a healthy mind and life.

They don't miss you as a person—they miss controlling and mistreating you. Narcissistic ex-partners only try to play the "let's be friends" card because they miss what you provide for them. They miss putting you down. They don't miss you as a person, because they truly can't wrap their heads around people as individual human beings. To them, supply is supply. They rarely know their sources of supply beyond a shallow impression of them as objects to control and misuse for their own gain. Remember that when a narcissistic abuser tries to come back to you, saying they miss you, what they're *really* saying is that they miss the power and control they feel when they are able to provoke your emotions. *They care about fulfilling their own needs.*

Empathic people leave their ex-partners alone and move forward, especially after they realize that an ex-partner is not the one for them. Narcissists don't care what is best for their ex-partner; they don't care if you're potentially retraumatized by their actions, such as reaching out to you or flaunting their new partner in front of you. They want to fulfill their own needs and it doesn't matter who they hurt in the process. Give yourself this reality check each and every time you find yourself romanticizing the abuser: they do not love or care about you in the way you deserve. If they did, they would have made the effort to treat you better. Love is expressed in actions, not empty words.

Reserve your energy and emotions for those who deserve it. You don't have to express and overexplain yourself to people who are committed to misunderstanding, invalidating, and mistreating you. Reserve your energy and time for people who are willing to see your beautiful strengths and celebrate them. Use your voice for people who truly want to help you, who appreciate your help and reciprocate your efforts.

Rather than wasting your precious efforts and empathy on people who are determined to silence or dismiss you, use it to help those who really need it, to comfort someone who is just as empathic and compassionate as you are, or to share your story and change the world. I guarantee you that helping people who are *actually able* to evolve (and this includes yourself!) is a much better use of your voice than trying to convince a person without empathy to treat you well. It's more likely to be effective, too.

Your mental health and self-care are your number one priorities. It's important to engage in extreme self-care during the "no contact" journey. This means checking in with yourself every moment of the day to ensure that you are thinking healthy thoughts, engaging in healthy patterns, taking advantage of the diverse healing modalities available to you as discussed previously, and addressing any symptoms of trauma that may be interfering with your ability to function in day-to-day life. If your mental health is suffering, all other aspects of your life will also feel the impact and it will be a domino effect across the board. So take care of yourself—and don't be afraid to seek professional support if you need it.

Your self-validation and sanity are far more important than being validated by an abuser who benefits from demeaning and controlling you. When you have been devalued by a toxic person, you can feel overwhelmed by the need to be validated by them as worthy, especially if they idealized you only to abruptly thrust you off the pedestal. This need becomes heightened when you see that the abuser seems to have moved on with a new partner. The narcissist was your source of a pervasive sense of unworthiness, so now you may feel as if you need confirmation from them that you are not the problem. Yet this sense of closure will evade you because of the narcissist's need for impression management. These types rarely fully share or disclose what is actually happening behind closed doors, so all you are likely to see is them love bombing and praising their next partner, just like they did with you. That's why you must prioritize your own sanity by accepting that you may never get a full sense of closure or confirmation of your worth from the narcissist. However, you can find ways of cultivating your self-belief as you move forward in your healing. This means stepping away from the narcissist's public façade and investing in living your own best, thriving life— one that, unlike the narcissist's life, is real and authentic in its joy and success.

You can trust your own reality. You know and can trust what you experienced and felt. It's important to ground yourself in your own reality and resist their gaslighting attempts to strengthen the trauma bond. It doesn't matter whether the narcissist or psychopath is on the cover of *Time* magazine for Person of the Year. Their popularity and public façade don't make them any less manipulative or callous. In fact, many malignant narcissists disguise themselves as charitable, loving people. That is the nature of their false mask: they are wolves in sheep's clothing.

This is to remind you that despite the amount of people your toxic partner has fooled, no one has the right to take away the reality of the abuse that you endured. You know what you have experienced—you know how valid it is and the impact it has left on you. It doesn't matter how charming the narcissistic abuser is or who chooses to believe them; let people learn at their own pace who the narcissist is. You're not here to convince anyone. You're here to validate yourself and resist the gaslighting attempts to distort your reality and that of the abuse. Don't feel obligated to protect the narcissist or minimize, rationalize, or deny their abuse. Honor and acknowledge your authentic emotions and the depth of trauma you have experienced.

You are worthy, attractive, brave, strong, and fearless. These are another set of positive affirmations that can help remind you of how worthy and courageous you truly are, with or without a partner. Positive affirmations condition you into believing good things about yourself, especially if you're used to hearing harsh words from your abuser. I recommend recording these and listening to them on a daily basis just to get yourself used to hearing them. Repetition is essential to deprogramming the harmful messages your abuser instilled in you and reprogramming your mind for future success.

Each second, each minute, each hour, each day, each month, each year, you are getting stronger. While you may have moments of weakness and hopelessness from time to time, rest assured that as you move forward with no contact, you will gain more and more strength and resilience than you ever knew was possible. As more time passes and as more trauma is processed and addressed, you'll carve out more space to become the person you are meant to be. You'll eventually reach a point in your healing journey where the strong attachment to the abusive person has dulled in its emotional potency.

Leaving a toxic relationship (or being left) is the best thing that will ever happen to you. You are a strong badass. You can survive anything, and you will thrive. It is the force of your personal strength and your powerful inner light that have gotten you through the worst moments of your life, so never underestimate your ability to survive and thrive after a toxic relationship. There are so many people still in abusive relationships. You've awakened and taken back control of your life. Do not take this blessing for granted. Instead of focusing on the ways you still feel trapped, validate your grief while celebrating your freedom. For every crucifixion, there is an even greater possibility for resurrection. Transform all your grief and outrage for the greater good: use it to fuel you to reach greater heights, achieve your goals, and kick some serious butt in all facets of your life.

Your success and healing are their karma. Karma can answer the narcissist—you will be too busy thriving from now on. You don't have to be vindictive or retaliate against your ex-partner in order to take care of yourself, set healthy boundaries, or live a victorious life. At the same time, you don't have to internalize anyone else's issues. You can empower yourself by establishing your boundaries and following through with them each and every time. The healing journey is all about becoming more grounded in your authentic truth.

Live your most empowering and abundant life and try to minimize your focus on what the narcissist is doing, who they are seeing, or what they are getting away with. Let people learn for themselves; you don't need to educate grown adults on how to be decent people. You don't need to give karma a "push" either—let it unfold organically.

You can lead a very successful life after a toxic relationship and move on to healthier, loving relationships as well. When you channel your experiences into your highest good, you will discover that the person you were once hyperfixated on and trauma bonded to no longer holds the same importance in your life. The best karma a narcissist can receive is actually the weight of your indifference and success after you have left them and broken the trauma bond for good.

Takeaways

You have now reached one of the most empowering stages of your journey as you finish this chapter. Congratulations! You are now armed with the skills to tackle challenges as you go no contact with narcissists, set healthy boundaries in love and dating, and overcome manipulation and exploitation in your relationships. I hope that this book has given you the knowledge and insight needed to break free from the trauma bonds and toxic people in your life and pave the path back to freedom and healing. You deserve the very best and you deserve to flourish.

Acknowledgments

I am so thankful to all the survivors who contributed to my research on this topic and for sharing their stories with me, as well as all the incredible readers who have been following my work for the past eight years. Thank you so much to my beautiful and brilliant mother, Rehana, who worked tirelessly as a math professor to make sure her children could pursue their dreams in America, and helped me become the avid learner, writer, and researcher I am today. I am eternally grateful to the New Harbinger team for strengthening this book and making it more accessible to a wider audience of readers: thank you so much to Jess O'Brien, Marisa Solis, Karen Levy, Jennifer Holder, and Amy Shoup, for believing in this book, and for all your amazing feedback and helpful support. Thank you to Jackson MacKenzie, who first paved the path to empowerment for survivors and who encouraged me to write for survivors from the very beginning—you will always be remembered. Thank you to every platform that has ever housed my work and allowed it to reach survivors, as well as every professor and mentor who has ever guided me in my work and professional journey. And finally, thank you to every reader of this book, for trusting me as a resource on your healing journey. You deserve the very best and the kindness you so generously give to others.

References

Abe, N., Greene, J. D., & Kiehl, K. A. (2018). Reduced engagement of the anterior cingulate cortex in the dishonest decision-making of incarcerated psychopaths. *Social Cognitive and Affective Neuroscience, 13*(8), 797–807. https://doi.org/10.1093/scan/nsy050

Adorjan, M., Christensen, T., Kelly, B., & Pawluch, D. (2012). Stockholm syndrome as vernacular resource. *The Sociological Quarterly, 53*(3), 454–474. https://doi.org/10.1111/j.1533-8525.2012.01241.x

Ali, F., Amorim, I. S., & Chamorro-Premuzic, T. (2009). Empathy deficits and trait emotional intelligence in psychopathy and Machiavellianism. *Personality and Individual Differences, 47*(7), 758–762. https://doi.org/10.1016/j.paid.2009.06.016

American Psychiatric Association. (2013). *Diagnostic and Statistical Manual of Mental Disorders* (5th ed.). Arlington, VA: American Psychiatric Publishing.

Anderson, N. E., & Kiehl, K. A. (2014). Psychopathy: Developmental perspectives and their implications for treatment. *Restorative Neurology and Neuroscience, 32*(1), 103–117. https://doi.org/10.3233/RNN-139001

Arabi, S. (2023). Narcissistic and psychopathic traits in romantic partners predict post-traumatic stress disorder symptomology: Evidence for unique impact in a large sample. *Personality and Individual Differences, 201*.

Aron, A., Melinat, E., Aron, E. N., Vallone, R. D., & Bator, R. J. (1997). The experimental generation of interpersonal closeness: A procedure and some preliminary findings. *Personality & Social Psychology Bulletin, 23*(4), 363–377. https://doi.org/10.1177/0146167297234003

Asmundson, G. J. G., Thorisdottir, A. S., Roden-Foreman, J. W., Baird, S. O., Witcraft, S. M., Stein, et al. (2019). A meta-analytic review of cognitive processing therapy for adults with posttraumatic stress disorder. *Cognitive Behaviour Therapy, 48*(1), 1–14. https://doi.org/10.1080/16506073.2018.1522371

Azizli, N., Atkinson, B. E., Baughman, H. M., Chin, K., Vernon, P. A., Harris, E., & Veselka, L. (2016). Lies and crimes: Dark Triad, misconduct, and high-stakes deception. *Personality and Individual Differences, 89*, 34–39. https://doi.org/10.1016/j.paid.2015.09.034

Bach, D., Groesbeck, G., Stapleton, P., Sims, R., Blickheuser, K., & Church, D. (2019). Clinical EFT (emotional freedom techniques) improves multiple physiological markers of health. *Journal of Evidence-Based Integrative Medicine, 24.*

Baik, J. H. (2020). Stress and the dopaminergic reward system. *Experimental and Molecular Medicine, 52,* 1879–1890.

Baldwin, S. B., Fehrenbacher, A. E., & Eisenman, D. P. (2015). Psychological coercion in human trafficking: An application of Biderman's framework. *Qualitative Health Research, 25*(9), 1171–1181. https://doi. org/10.1177/1049732314557087

Baughman, H. M., Jonason, P. K., Lyons, M., & Vernon, P. A. (2014). Liar liar pants on fire: Cheater strategies linked to the Dark Triad. *Personality and Individual Differences, 71,* 35–38. https://doi.org/10.1016/j.paid.2014.07.019

Beck, J. S., & Fleming, S. (2021). A brief history of Aaron T. Beck, MD, and cognitive behavior therapy. *Clinical Psychology in Europe, 3*(2), e6701. https://doi.org/10.32872/cpe.6701

Bedard-Gilligan, M., & Zoellner, L. A. (2012). Dissociation and memory fragmentation in posttraumatic stress disorder: An evaluation of the dissociative encoding hypothesis. *Memory, 20*(3), 277-299. https://doi.org/10.10 80/09658211.2012.655747

Begni, V., Riva, M. A., & Cattaneo, A. (2017). Cellular and molecular mechanisms of the brain-derived neurotrophic factor in physiological and pathological conditions. *Clinical Science, 131*(2), 123–138. https://doi.org/10.1042/ CS20160009

Belleau E. L., Ehret, L. E., Hanson, J. L., Brasel, K. J., Larson, C. L., & deRoon-Cassini, T. A. (2020). Amygdala functional connectivity in the acute aftermath of trauma prospectively predicts severity of posttraumatic stress symptoms. *Neurobiology of Stress, 12.* https://doi.org/10.1016/j.ynstr.2020.100217

Benning, S. D., Patrick, C. J., & Iacono, W. G. (2005). Psychopathy, startle blink modulation, and electrodermal reactivity in twin men. *Psychophysiology, 42*(6), 753–762. https://doi.org/10.1111/j.1469-8986 .2005.00353.x

Böger, A., & Huxhold, O. (2020). The changing relationship between partnership status and loneliness: Effects related to aging and historical time. *The Journals of Gerontology: Series B: Psychological Sciences and Social Sciences, 75*(7), 1423–1432.

Boyd, J. E., Lanius, R. A., & McKinnon, M. C. (2018). Mindfulness-based treatments for posttraumatic stress disorder: a review of the treatment literature and neurobiological evidence. *Journal of Psychiatry & Neuroscience, 43*(1), 7–25.

Blair, R. J. (2013). The neurobiology of psychopathic traits in youths. *Nature Reviews: Neuroscience, 14*(11), 786–799. https://doi.org/10.1038/nrn3577

Bremner, J. D. (2006). Traumatic stress: Effects on the brain. *Dialogues in Clinical Neuroscience, 8*(4), 445–461. https://doi.org/10.31887/dcns.2006.8.4/jbremner

Brenner, E. G., Schwartz, R. C., & Becker, C. (2023). Development of the internal family systems model: Honoring contributions from family systems therapies. *Family Process, 62*(4), 1290–1306. https://doi.org/10.1111/famp.12943

Brummelman, E., Thomaes, S., Nelemans, S. A., Orobio de Castro, B., Overbeek, G., & Bushman, B. J. (2015). Origins of narcissism in children. *Proceedings of the National Academy of Sciences of the United States of America, 112*(12), 3659–3662. https://doi.org/10.1073/pnas.1420870112

Buckholtz, J. W., Treadway, M. T., Cowan, R. L., Woodward, N. D., Benning, S. D., Li, R., et al. (2010). Mesolimbic dopamine reward system hypersensitivity in individuals with psychopathic traits. *Nature Neuroscience, 13*(4), 419–421. https://doi.org/10.1038/nn.2510

Cacioppo, S., & Cacioppo, J. (2016). Research in social neuroscience: How perceived social isolation, ostracism, and romantic rejection affect our brain. In P. Riva & J. Eck (Eds.), *Social Exclusion* (pp. 73–88). Cham, Switzerland: Springer International Publishing.

Cantor, C., & Price, J. (2007). Traumatic entrapment, appeasement and complex post-traumatic stress disorder: Evolutionary perspectives of hostage reactions, domestic abuse and the Stockholm syndrome. *The Australian and New Zealand Journal of Psychiatry, 41*(5), 377–384. https://doi.org/10.1080/00048670701261178

Carlson, E. N., Vazire, S., & Oltmanns, T. F. (2013). Self-other knowledge asymmetries in personality pathology. *Journal of Personality, 81*(2), 155–170. https://doi.org/10.1111/j.1467-6494.2012.00794.x

Carnes, P. J. (2019). *Betrayal Bond, Revised: Breaking Free of Exploitive Relationships.* Deerfield Beach, FL: Health Communications.

Carver, J. M. (2014). *Stockholm syndrome: The psychological mystery of loving an abuser.* Counselling Resource, December 20. https://counsellingresource.com/therapy/self-help/stockholm

Casassa, K., Knight, L., & Mengo, C. (2022). Trauma bonding perspectives from service providers and survivors of sex trafficking: A scoping review. *Trauma, Violence, & Abuse, 23*(3), 969–984.

Cascio, C. N., Konrath, S. H., & Falk, E. B. (2015). Narcissists' social pain seen only in the brain. *Social Cognitive and Affective Neuroscience, 10*(3), 335–341.

Castro, D. C., & Berridge, K. C. (2017). Opioid and orexin hedonic hotspots in rat orbitofrontal cortex and insula. *Proceedings of the National Academy of Sciences of the United States of America, 114*(43), E9125–E9134.

Chester, D. S., & DeWall, C. N. (2016). Sound the alarm: The effect of narcissism on retaliatory aggression is moderated by dACC reactivity to rejection. *Journal of Personality, 84*(3), 361–368.

Chester, D. S., Lynam, D. R., Powell, D. K., & DeWall, C. N. (2016). Narcissism is associated with weakened frontostriatal connectivity: A DTI study. *Social Cognitive and Affective Neuroscience, 11*(7), 1036–1040.

Cima, M., Tonnaer, F., & Hauser, M. D. (2010). Psychopaths know right from wrong but don't care. *Social Cognitive and Affective Neuroscience, 5*(1), 59–67. https://doi.org/10.1093/scan/nsp051

Clark, D. A., & Beck, A. T. (2010). *Cognitive Therapy of Anxiety Disorders: Science and Practice*. New York: Guilford Press.

Collinge, W., Kahn, J., Walton, T., Kozak, L., Bauer-Wu, S., Fletcher, K., Yarnold, P., & Soltysik, R. (2013). Touch, caring, and cancer: Randomized controlled trial of a multimedia caregiver education program. *Supportive Care in Cancer, 21*(5), 1405–1414. https://doi.org/10.1007/s00520-012-1682-6

Cope, L. M., Vincent, G. M., Jobelius, J. L., Nyalakanti, P. K., Calhoun, V. D., & Kiehl, K. A. (2014). Psychopathic traits modulate brain responses to drug cues in incarcerated offenders. *Frontiers in Human Neuroscience, 8*, 87. https://doi.org/10.3389/fnhum.2014.00087

Costa, M., Lozano-Soldevilla, D., Gil-Nagel, A., Toledano, R., Oehrn, C. R., Kunz, L., et al. (2022). Aversive memory formation in humans involves an amygdala-hippocampus phase code. *Nature Commununications, 13*, 6403. https://doi.org/10.1038/s41467-022-33828-2

Creswell, J. D., Lindsay, E. K., Villalba, D. K., & Chin, B. (2019). Mindfulness training and physical health: Mechanisms and outcomes. *Psychosomatic Medicine, 81*(3), 224–232.

Czarna, A. Z., Wróbel, M., Dufner, M., & Zeigler-Hill, V. (2015). Narcissism and emotional contagion: Do narcissists "catch" the emotions of others? *Social Psychological and Personality Science, 6*(3), 318–324.

Decety, J., Chen, C., Harenski, C., & Kiehl, K. A. (2013). An fMRI study of affective perspective taking in individuals with psychopathy: Imagining another in pain does not evoke empathy. *Frontiers in Human Neuroscience, 7*, 489. https://doi.org/10.3389/fnhum.2013.00489

Deming, P., Dargis, M., Haas, B. W., Brook, M., Decety, J., Harenski, C., Kiehl, K. A., Koenigs, M., & Kosson, D. S. (2020). Psychopathy is associated with fear-specific reductions in neural activity during affective perspective-taking. *NeuroImage, 223*, 117342.

DePaulo, B. (2023). Single and flourishing: Transcending the deficit narratives of single life. *Journal of Family Theory & Review, 15*(3), 389–411.

DeWall, C. N., Gillath, O., Pressman, S. D., Black, L. L., Bartz, J. A., Moskovitz, J., & Stetler, D. A. (2014). When the love hormone leads to violence: Oxytocin increases intimate partner violence inclinations among high trait aggressive people. *Social Psychological and Personality Science, 5*(6), 691–697.

Dixon, B. (2022). How to hack your brain, according to a neuroscientist. *Inc,* December 15. https://www.inc.com/video/how-to-hack-your-brain-according-to-a-neuroscientist.html

Dragioti, E., Damigos, D., Mavreas, V., & Gouva, M. (2012). Effects of childhood trauma on hostility, family environment and narcissism of adult individuals. *International Journal of Caring Sciences, 5*(2), 137-146.

Dutton, D. G., & Painter, S. (1993). Emotional attachments in abusive relationships: A test of traumatic bonding theory. *Violence and Victims, 8*(2), 105–120. https://doi.org/10.1891/0886-6708.8.2.105

Earp, B., Wudarczyk O., Foddy, B., & Savulescu, J. (2017). Addicted to love: What is love addiction and when should it be treated? *Philosophy, Psychiatry, & Psychology, 24*(1), 77–92. https://doi.org/10.1353/ppp.2017.0011

Eisenbarth, H., Godinez, D., du Pont, A., Corley, R. P., Stallings, M. C., & Rhee, S. H. (2019). The influence of stressful life events, psychopathy, and their interaction on internalizing and externalizing psychopathology. *Psychiatry Research, 272,* 438–446. Https://doi.org/10.1016/j.psychres.2018.12.145

Elliott, A. E., & Packard, M. G. (2008). Intra-amygdala anxiogenic drug infusion prior to retrieval biases rats towards the use of habit memory. *Neurobiology of Learning and Memory, 90*(4), 616–623. https://doi.org/10.1016/j.nlm.2008.06.012

Engel, C. C., Cordova, E. H., Benedek, D. M., Liu, X., Gore, K. L., Goertz, C., Freed, M. C., Crawford, C., Jonas, W. B., & Ursano, R. J. (2014). Randomized effectiveness trial of a brief course of acupuncture for posttraumatic stress disorder. *Medical Care, 52*(12 Suppl 5), S57–S64. https://doi.org/10.1097/MLR.0000000000000237

Ermer, E., Cope, L. M., Nyalakanti, P. K., Calhoun, V. D., & Kiehl, K. A. (2012). Aberrant paralimbic gray matter in criminal psychopathy. *Journal of Abnormal Psychology, 121*(3), 649–658.

Etkin, A., & Wager, T. D. (2007). Functional neuroimaging of anxiety: A meta-analysis of emotional processing in PTSD, social anxiety disorder, and specific phobia. *The American Journal of Psychiatry, 164*(10), 1476–1488. https://doi.org/10.1176/appi.ajp.2007.07030504

Ewert, A., & Chang, Y. (2018). Levels of nature and stress response. *Behavioral Sciences, 8*(5), 49.

Fan, Y., Wonneberger, C., Enzi, B., de Greck, M., Ulrich, C., Tempelmann, C., Bogerts, B., Doering, S., & Northoff, G. (2011). The narcissistic self and its psychological and neural correlates: An exploratory fMRI study. *Psychological Medicine, 41*(8), 1641–1650. https://doi.org/10.1017/S003329171000228X

Feng, C., Yuan, J., Geng, H., Gu, R., Zhou, H., Wu, X., & Luo, Y. (2018). Individualized prediction of trait narcissism from whole-brain resting-state functional connectivity. *Human Brain Mapping, 39*(9), 3701–3712. https://doi.org/10.1002/hbm.24205

Field, T., Hernandez-Reif, M., Diego, M., Schanberg, S., & Kuhn, C. (2005). Cortisol decreases and serotonin and dopamine increase following massage therapy. *The International Journal of Neuroscience, 115*(10), 1397–1413. https://doi.org/10.1080/00207450590956459

Fine, A. H., Beck, A. M., & Ng, Z. (2019). The state of animal-assisted interventions: Addressing the contemporary issues that will shape the future. *International Journal of Environmental Research and Public Health, 16*(20), 3997. https://doi.org/10.3390/ijerph16203997

Fisher, H. E., Aron, A., & Brown, L. L. (2006). Romantic love: A mammalian brain system for mate choice. *Philosophical Transactions of the Royal Society of London, 361*(1476), 2173–2186. https://doi.org/10.1098/rstb.2006.1938

Fisher, H. E., Xu, X., Aron, A., & Brown, L. L. (2016). Intense, passionate, romantic love: A natural addiction? How the fields that investigate romance and substance abuse can inform each other. *Frontiers in Psychology, 7*, 687. https://doi.org/10.3389/fpsyg.2016.00687

Freyd, J. J. (2008). Betrayal trauma. In G. Reyes, J. D. Elhai, & J. D Ford (Eds.), *Encyclopedia of Psychological Trauma* (p. 76). New York: John Wiley & Sons.

Gerra, G., Zaimovic, A., Moi, G., Bussandri, M., Delsignore, R., Caccavari, R., & Brambilla, F. (2003). Neuroendocrine correlates of antisocial personality disorder in abstinent heroin-dependent subjects. *Addiction Biology, 8*(1), 23–32. https://10.1080/1355621031000069846

Goldsby, T. L., & Goldsby, M. E. (2020). Eastern integrative medicine and ancient sound healing treatments for stress: Recent research advances. *Integrative Medicine, 19*(6), 24–30.

Gómez, J. M., & Freyd, J. J. (2019). Betrayal trauma. In J. J. Ponzetti (Ed.), *Macmillan encyclopedia of intimate and family relationships: An interdisciplinary approach* (pp. 79–82). Boston, MA: Cengage Learning.

Gong, X., Brazil, I.A., Chang, L.J., & Sanfey, A. G. (2019). Psychopathic traits are related to diminished guilt aversion and reduced trustworthiness during social decision-making. *Scientific Reports, 9*, 7307. https://doi.org/10.1038/s41598-019-43727-0

Gottman, J., & Silver, N. (1999). *The Seven Principles for Making Marriage Work*. New York: Crown Publishers.

Grijalva, E., & Zhang, L. (2016). Narcissism and self-insight: A review and meta-analysis of narcissists' self-enhancement tendencies. *Personality and Social Psychology Bulletin, 42*(1), 3–24. https://doi.org/10.1177/0146167215611636

Guidi, J., Lucente, M., Sonino, N., & Fava, G. A. (2021). Allostatic load and its impact on health: A systematic review. *Psychotherapy and Psychosomatics, 90*(1), 11–27. https://doi.org/10.1159/000510696

Hare, R. D., & Neumann, C. S. (2005). Structural models of psychopathy. *Current Psychiatry Reports, 7*(1), 57–64. https://doi.org/10.1007/s11920-005-0026-3

Harenski, C. L., Harenski, K. A., Shane, M. S., & Kiehl, K. A. (2010). Aberrant neural processing of moral violations in criminal psychopaths. *Journal of Abnormal Psychology, 119*(4), 863–874. https://doi.org/10.1037/a0020979

Hediger, K., Wagner, J., Künzi, P., Haefeli, A., Theis, F., Grob, C., Pauli, E., & Gerger, H. (2021). Effectiveness of animal-assisted interventions for children and adults with post-traumatic stress disorder symptoms: A systematic review and meta-analysis. *European Journal of Psychotraumatology, 12*(1), 1879713.

Hill, M. D. (2020). Adaptive information processing theory: Origins, principles, applications, and evidence. *Journal of Evidence-Based Social Work, 17*(3), 317–331. https://doi.org/10.1080/26408066.2020.1748155

Hölzel, B. K., Carmody, J., Evans, K. C., Hoge, E. A., Dusek, J. A., Morgan, L., et al. (2010). Stress reduction correlates with structural changes in the amygdala. *Social Cognitive and Affective Neuroscience, 5*(1), 11–17. https://doi.org/10.1093/scan/nsp034

Hölzel, B. K., Carmody, J., Vangel, M., Congleton, C., Yerramsetti, S. M., Gard, T., & Lazar, S. W. (2011). Mindfulness practice leads to increases in regional brain gray matter density. *Psychiatry Research, 191*(1), 36–43. https://doi.org/10.1016/j.pscychresns.2010.08.006

Horan, S., Guinn, T., & Banghart, S. (2015). Understanding relationships among the Dark Triad personality profile and romantic partners' conflict communication. *Communication Quarterly, 63*(2), 156–170.

Jauk, E., Benedek, M., Koschutnig, K., Kedia, G., & Neubauer, A. C. (2017). Self-viewing is associated with negative affect rather than reward in highly narcissistic men: An fMRI study. *Scientific Reports, 7*, 5804. https://doi.org/10.1038/s41598-017-03935-y

Jauk, E., & Kanske, P. (2021). Can neuroscience help to understand narcissism? A systematic review of an emerging field. *Personality Neuroscience, 4*, e3. https://doi.org/10.1017/pen.2021.1

Johnson-Freyd, S., & Freyd, J. J. (2013). Revenge and forgiveness or betrayal blindness? *The Behavioral and Brain Sciences, 36*(1), 23–24. https://doi.org/10.1017/S0140525X12000398

Jonason, P. K., Lyons, M., Baughman, H. M., & Vernon, P. A. (2014). What a tangled web we weave: The Dark Triad traits and deception. *Personality and Individual Differences, 70*, 117–119. https://doi.org/10.1016/j.paid.2014.06.038

Jones, R. M., Somerville, L. H., Li, J., Ruberry, E. J., Libby, V., Glover, G., Voss, H. U., Ballon, D. J., & Casey, B. J. (2011). Behavioral and neural properties of social reinforcement learning. *Journal of Neuroscience, 31*(37), 13039–13045. https://doi.org/10.1523/jneurosci.2972-11.2011

Kalmijn, M. (2017). The ambiguous link between marriage and health: A dynamic reanalysis of loss and gain effects. *Social Forces, 95*(4), 1607–1636. https://doi.org/10.1093/sf/sox015

Kelsey, R. M., Ornduff, S. R., McCann, C. M., & Reiff, S. (2001). Psychophysiological characteristics of narcissism during active and passive coping. *Psychophysiology, 38*(2), 292–303.

Kiehl, K. A., Smith, A. M., Hare, R. D., Mendrek, A., Forster, B. B., Brink, J., & Liddle, P. F. (2001). Limbic abnormalities in affective processing by criminal psychopaths as revealed by functional magnetic resonance imaging. *Biological Psychiatry, 50*(9), 677–684. https://doi.org/10.1016/s0006-3223(01)01222-7

King, D. (2020). A 1973 bank robbery gave the world "Stockholm syndrome"—But there's more to the story than that. *Time*, August 4. https://time.com/5874808/stockholm-syndrome-history

Kim, S.-Y., Adhikari, A., Lee, S. Y., Marshel, J. H., Kim, C. K., Mallory, C. S., Lo, M., et al. (2013). Diverging neural pathways assemble a behavioural state from separable features in anxiety. *Nature 496*, 219–223. https://doi.org/10.1038/nature12018

Kimonis, E. R., Frick, P. J., Cauffman, E., Goldweber, A., & Skeem, J. (2012). Primary and secondary variants of juvenile psychopathy differ in emotional processing. *Development and Psychopathology, 24*(3), 1091–1103.

Kjærvik, S. L., & Bushman, B. J. (2021). The link between narcissism and aggression: A meta-analytic review. *Psychological Bulletin, 147*(5), 477–503. https://doi.org/10.1037/bul0000323

Kwon, C. Y., Lee, B., & Kim, S. H. (2021). Efficacy and underlying mechanism of acupuncture in the treatment of posttraumatic stress disorder: A systematic review of animal studies. *Journal of Clinical Medicine, 10*(8), 1575. http://doi.org/10.3390/jcm10081575

Koenigs, M. (2012). The role of prefrontal cortex in psychopathy. *Reviews in the Neurosciences, 23*(3), 253–262. https://doi.org/10.1515/revneuro-2012-0036

Lange, J., Crusius, J., & Hagemeyer, B. (2016). The evil queen's dilemma: Linking narcissistic admiration and rivalry to benign and malicious envy. *European Journal of Personality, 30*(2), 168–188. https://doi.org/10.1002/per.2047

Lange, J., Paulhus, D. L., & Crusius, J. (2018). Elucidating the dark side of envy: Distinctive links of benign and malicious envy with dark personalities. *Personality & Social Psychology Bulletin, 44*(4), 601–614. https://doi.org/10.1177/0146167217746340

Langeslag, S., van der Veen, F., & Fekkes, D. (2012). Blood levels of serotonin are differentially affected by romantic love in men and women. *Journal of Psychophysiology, 26*(2), 92–98.

Laplaud, N., Perrochon, A., Gallou-Guyot, M., Moens, M., Goudman, L., David, R., Rigoard, P., & Billot, M. (2023). Management of post-traumatic stress disorder symptoms by yoga: An overview. *BMC Complementary Medicine and Therapies, 23*(1), 258.

Leedom, L. J., Andersen, D. M., Glynn, M. A., & Barone, M. L. (2019). Counseling intimate partner abuse survivors: Effective and ineffective interventions. *Journal of Counseling & Development, 94*(4), 364–375.

Lenzenweger, M. F., Clarkin, J. F., Caligor, E., Cain, N. M., & Kernberg, O. F. (2018). Malignant narcissism in relation to clinical change in borderline personality disorder: An exploratory study. *Psychopathology, 51*(5), 318–325. https://doi.org/10.1159/000492228

Luhmann, M., Hofmann, W., Eid, M., & Lucas, R. E. (2012). Subjective well-being and adaptation to life events: A meta-analysis. *Journal of Personality and Social Psychology, 102*(3), 592–615.

Mao, Y., Sang, N., Wang, Y., Hou, X., Huang, H., Wei, D., Zhang, J., & Qiu, J. (2016). Reduced frontal cortex thickness and cortical volume associated with pathological narcissism. *Neuroscience, 328*, 50–57. https://doi.org/10.1016/j.neuroscience.2016.04.025

Marazziti, D., Akiskal, H. S., Rossi, A., & Cassano, G. B. (1999). Alteration of the platelet serotonin transporter in romantic love. *Psychological Medicine, 29*(3), 741–745.

Marazziti, D., & Canale, D. (2004). Hormonal changes when falling in love. *Psychoneuroendocrinology, 29*(7), 931–936. https://10.1016/j.psyneuen.2003.08.006

Marazziti, D., & Stahl, S. M. (2018). Serotonin and love: Supporting evidence from a patient suffering from obsessive-compulsive disorder. *Journal of Clinical Psychopharmacology, 38*(1), 99–101. http://doi.org10.1097/JCP.0000000000000808.

Massar, K., Winters, C. L., Lenz, S., & Jonason, P. K. (2017). Green-eyed snakes: The associations between psychopathy, jealousy, and jealousy induction. *Personality and Individual Differences, 115*, 164–168.

May, J. M., Richardi, T. M., & Barth, K. S. (2016). Dialectical behavior therapy as treatment for borderline personality disorder. *The Mental Health Clinician, 6*(2), 62–67. https://doi.org/10.9740/mhc.2016.03.62

McKay, M., Wood, J., & Brantley, J. (2021). *The Dialectical Behavior Therapy Skills Workbook: Practical DBT Exercises for Learning Mindfulness, Interpersonal Effectiveness, and Emotion Regulation.* Oakland, CA: New Harbinger Publications.

McLean, C. P., Levy, H. C., Miller, M. L., & Tolin, D. F. (2022). Exposure therapy for PTSD: A meta-analysis. *Clinical Psychology Review, 91*, 102115. https://doi.org/10.1016/j.cpr.2021.102115

McManus, S., Walby, S., Barbosa, E. C., Appleby, L., Brugha, T., Bebbington, P. E., Cook, E. A., & Knipe, D. (2022). Intimate partner violence, suicidality, and self-harm: A probability sample survey of the general population in England. *The Lancet: Psychiatry, 9*(7), 574–583. https://doi.org/10.1016/S2215-0366(22)00151-1

Miller, J. D., Pilkonis, P. A., & Clifton, A. (2005). Self- and other-reports of traits from the five-factor model: Relations to personality disorder. *Journal of Personality Disorders, 19*(4), 400–419. https://doi.org/10.1521/pedi.2005.19.4.400

Mims, D., & Waddell, R. (2016). Animal assisted therapy and trauma survivors. *Journal of Evidence-Informed Social Work, 13*(5), 452–457. https://doi.org/10.1080/23761407.2016.1166841

Miranda, M., Morici, J. F., Zanoni, M. B., & Bekinschtein, P. (2019). Brain-derived neurotrophic factor: A key molecule for memory in the healthy and the pathological brain. *Frontiers in Cellular Neuroscience, 13*, 363. https://doi.org/10.3389/fncel.2019.00363

Nakao, M., Shirotsuki, K., & Sugaya, N. (2021). Cognitive-behavioral therapy for management of mental health and stress-related disorders: Recent advances in techniques and technologies. *BioPsychoSocial Medicine, 15*(1), 16. https://doi.org/10.1186/s13030-021-00219-w

Nenadic, I., Güllmar, D., Dietzek, M., Langbein, K., Steinke, J., & Gaser, C. (2015). Brain structure in narcissistic personality disorder: A VBM and DTI pilot study. *Psychiatry Research, 231*(2), 184–186.

Ozer, E. J., Best, S. R., Lipsey, T. L., & Weiss, D. S. (2003). Predictors of posttraumatic stress disorder and symptoms in adults: A meta-analysis. *Psychological Bulletin, 129*(1), 52-73. https://doi.org/10.1037/0033-2909.129.1.52

Pant, U., Frishkopf, M., Park, T., Norris, C. M., & Papathanassoglou, E. (2022). A neurobiological framework for the therapeutic potential of music and sound interventions for post-traumatic stress symptoms in critical illness survivors. *International Journal of Environmental Research and Public Health, 19*(5), 3113. https://doi.org/10.3390/ijerph19053113

Papageorgiou, K. A., Gianniou, F.-M., Wilson, P., Moneta, G. B., Bilello, D., & Clough, P. J. (2019). The bright side of dark: Exploring the positive effect of narcissism on perceived stress through mental toughness. *Personality and Individual Differences, 139*, 116–124. https://doi.org/10.1016/j.paid.2018.11.004

Park, S. W., & Colvin, C. R. (2014). Narcissism and other-derogation in the absence of ego threat. *Journal of Personality, 83*(3), 334–345. https://doi.org/10.1111/jopy.12107

Patrick, C. J., Bradley, M. M., & Lang, P. J. (1993). Emotion in the criminal psychopath: Startle reflex modulation. *Journal of Abnormal Psychology, 102*(1), 82–92. https://doi.org/10.1037/0021-843X.102.1.82

Perl, O., Duek, O., Kulkarni, K. R., Gordon, C., Krystal, J. H., Levy, I., et al. (2023). Neural patterns differentiate traumatic from sad autobiographical memories in PTSD. *Nature Neuroscience, 26*, 2226-2236. https://doi.org/10.1038/s41593-023-01483-5

Reid, J. A., Haskell, R. A., Dillahunt-Aspillaga, C., Thor, J. A. (2013). Contemporary review of empirical and clinical studies of trauma bonding in violent or exploitative relationships. *International Journal of Psychology Research, 8*(1), 37–73.

Reidy, D. E., Kearns, M. C., & DeGue, S. (2013). Reducing psychopathic violence: A review of the treatment literature. *Aggression and Violent Behavior, 18*(5), 527–538. https://doi.org/10.1016/j.avb.2013.07.008

Reinhardt, T., Schmahl, C., Wüst, S., & Bohus, M. (2012). Salivary cortisol, heart rate, electrodermal activity and subjective stress responses to the Mannheim Multicomponent Stress Test (MMST). *Psychiatry Research, 198*(1), 106–111. https://doi.org/10.1016/j.psychres.2011.12.009

Rhodes, A., Spinazzola, J., & van der Kolk, B. (2016). Yoga for adult women with chronic PTSD: A long-term follow-up study. *Journal of Alternative and Complementary Medicine, 22*(3), 189–196. https://doi.org/10.1089/acm.2014.0407

Rilling, J. K., Glenn, A. L., Jairam, M. R., Pagnoni, G., Goldsmith, D. R., Elfenbein, H. A., & Lilienfeld, S. O. (2007). Neural correlates of social cooperation and non-cooperation as a function of psychopathy. *Biological Psychiatry, 61*(11), 1260–1271. https://doi.org/10.1016/j.biopsych.2006.07.021

Ronningstam, E., & Baskin-Sommers, A. R. (2013). Fear and decision-making in narcissistic personality disorder: A link between psychoanalysis and neuroscience. *Dialogues in Clinical Neuroscience, 15*(2), 191–201. https://doi.org/10.31887/DCNS.2013.15.2/eronningstam

Saltoğlu, S., & Uysal Irak, D. (2022). Primary versus secondary psychopathy: Coping styles as a mediator between psychopathy and well-being. *Current Psychology, 41*(9), 6534–6542.

Schulze, L., Dziobek, I., Vater, A., Heekeren, H. R., Bajbouj, M., Renneberg, B., Heuser, I., & Roepke, S. (2013). Gray matter abnormalities in patients with narcissistic personality disorder. *Journal of Psychiatric Research, 47*(10), 1363–1369. https://doi.org/10.1016/j.jpsychires.2013.05.017

Seara-Cardoso, A., & Viding, E. (2015). Functional neuroscience of psychopathic personality in adults. *Journal of Personality, 83*(6), 723–737. https://doi.org/10.1111/jopy.12113

Seara-Cardoso, A., Sebastian, C. L., Viding, E., & Roiser, J. P. (2016). Affective resonance in response to others' emotional faces varies with affective ratings and psychopathic traits in amygdala and anterior insula. *Social Neuroscience, 11*(2), 140–152. https://doi.org/10.1080/17470919.2015.1044672

Seshadri, K. G. (2016). The neuroendocrinology of love. *Indian Journal of Endocrinology and Metabolism, 20*(4), 558–563. https://doi.org/10.4103/2230-8210.183479

Sethi, A., McCrory, E., Puetz, V., Hoffmann, F., Knodt, A. R., Radtke, S. R., Brigidi, B. D., Hariri, A. R., & Viding, E. (2018). Primary and secondary variants of psychopathy in a volunteer sample are associated with different neurocognitive mechanisms. *Biological Psychiatry: Cognitive Neuroscience and Neuroimaging, 3*(12): 1013–1021. 10.1016/j.bpsc.2018.04.002

Shapiro, F. (1990). Eye movement desensitization procedure: A new treatment for anxiety and related traumata. *California Psychologist, 18–19.*

Shih, H.-C., Kuo, M.-E., Wu, C. W., Chao, Y.-P., Huang, H.-W., & Huang, C.-M. (2022). The neurobiological basis of love: A meta-analysis of human functional neuroimaging studies of maternal and passionate love. *Brain Sciences, 12*(7), 830. https://doi.org/10.3390/brainsci12070830

Shin, L. M., Rauch, S. L., & Pitman, R. K. (2006). Amygdala, medial prefrontal cortex, and hippocampal function in PTSD. *Annals of the New York Academy of Sciences, 1071,* 67–79. https://doi.org/10.1196/annals.1364.007

Sleiman, S. F., Henry, J., Al-Haddad, R., El Hayek, L., Abou Haidar, E., Stringer, T., et al. (2016). Exercise promotes the expression of brain derived neurotrophic factor (BDNF) through the action of the ketone body β-hydroxybutyrate. *eLife, 5,* e15092. https://doi.org/10.7554/eLife.15092

Sorokowski, P., Żelaźniewicz, A., Nowak, J., Groyecka, A., Kaleta, M., Lech, W., et al. (2019). Romantic love and reproductive hormones in women. *International Journal of Environmental Research and Public Health, 16*(21), 4224. https://doi.org/10.3390/ijerph16214224

Stephenson-Jones, M., Bravo-Rivera, C., Ahrens, S., Furlan, A., Xiao, X., Fernandes-Henriques, C., & Li, B. (2020). Opposing contributions of GABAergic and glutamatergic ventral pallidal neurons to motivational behaviors. *Neuron, 105*(5), 921–933.e5. https://doi.org/10.1016/j.neuron.2019.12.006

Strutzenberg, C. C., Wiersma-Mosley, J. D., Jozkowski, K. N., & Becnel, J. N. (2017). Love-bombing: A narcissistic approach to relationship formation. *Discovery: The Journal of Dale Bumpers College of Agricultural, Food and Life Sciences, 18*(1), 81–89.

Takayanagi, Y., & Onaka, T. (2021). Roles of oxytocin in stress responses, allostasis and resilience. *International Journal of Molecular Sciences, 23*(1), 150. https://doi.org/10.3390/ijms23010150

Tang, R., Friston, K. J., & Tang, Y. Y. (2020). Brief mindfulness meditation induces gray matter changes in a brain hub. *Neural Plasticity, 2020,* 8830005. https://doi.org/10.1155/2020/8830005

Tang, X., Lin, S., Fang, D., Lin, B., Yao, L., Wang, L., Xu, Q., Lu, L., & Xu, N. (2023). Efficacy and underlying mechanisms of acupuncture therapy for PTSD: Evidence from animal and clinical studies. *Frontiers in Behavioral Neuroscience, 17,* 1163718. https://doi.org/10.3389/fnbeh.2023.1163718

Tatar, J. R., Cauffman, E., Kimonis, E. R., & Skeem, J. L. (2012). Victimization history and posttraumatic stress: An analysis of psychopathy variants in male juvenile offenders. *Journal of Child & Adolescent Trauma, 5*(2): 102–113, https://doi.org/10.1037/a0028047

Taylor, J., McLean, L., Korner, A., Stratton, E., & Glozier, N. (2020). Mindfulness and yoga for psychological trauma: Systematic review and meta-analysis. *Journal of Trauma & Dissociation, 21*(5), 536–573. https://doi.org/10.1080/15299732.2020.1760167

Tortoriello, G. K., Hart, W., Richardson, K., & Tullett, A. M. (2017). Do narcissists try to make romantic partners jealous on purpose? An examination of motives for deliberate jealousy-induction among subtypes of narcissism. *Personality and Individual Differences, 114,* 10–15. https://doi.org/10.1016/j.paid.2017.03.052

Tumin, D., & Zheng, H. (2018). Do the health benefits of marriage depend on the likelihood of marriage? *Journal of Marriage and Family, 80*(3), 622–636. https://doi.org/10.1111/jomf.12471

Uzieblo, K., Soetens, B., & Bijttebier, P. (2011). The fatal partner: Psychopathy and its effects on the psychosocial and relational well-being of the partner. Presentation at the Biennial Meeting of the Society for the Scientific Study of Psychopathy, Montréal, Canada.

van Schie, C. C., Jarman, H. L., Huxley, E., & Grenyer, B. F. S. (2020). Narcissistic traits in young people: Understanding the role of parenting and maltreatment. *Borderline Personality Disorder and Emotion Dysregulation, 7,* 10. https://doi.org/10.1186/s40479-020-00125-7

Vincent, G. M., Cope, L. M., King, J., Nyalakanti, P., & Kiehl, K. A. (2018). Callous-unemotional traits modulate brain drug craving response in high-risk young offenders. *Journal of Abnormal Child Psychology, 46*(5), 993–1009. https://doi.org/10.1007/s10802-017-0364-8

Wai, M., & Tiliopoulos, N. (2012). The affective and cognitive empathic nature of the dark triad of personality. *Personality and Individual Differences, 52*(7), 794–799. https://doi.org/10.1016/j.paid.2012.01.008

Wallace, P. (2007). How can she still love him? Domestic violence and the Stockholm syndrome. *Community Practitioner, 80*(10), 32–34.

Weisman, O., Schneiderman, I., Zagoory-Sharon, O., & Feldman, R. (2014). Early-stage romantic love is associated with reduced daily cortisol production. *Adaptive Human Behavior and Physiology, 1*(1), 41–53.

Worthen-Chaudhari, L. (2021). Clinical trial of a rehabilitation game: SuperBetter. *National Library of Medicine.* https://classic.clinicaltrials.gov/ct2/history/NCT01398566

Zald, D. H., Boileau, I., El-Dearedy, W., Gunn, R., McGlone, F., Dichter, G. S., & Dagher, A. (2004). Dopamine transmission in the human striatum during monetary reward tasks. *The Journal of Neuroscience, 24*(17), 4105–4112. https://doi.org/10.1523/JNEUROSCI.4643-03.2004

Zak, P. J., Kurzban, R., & Matzner, W. T. (2005). Oxytocin is associated with human trustworthiness. *Hormones and Behavior, 48*(5), 522–527. https://doi.org/10.1016/j.yhbeh.2005.07.009

Zalta, A. K., Held, P., Smith, D. L., Klassen, B. J., Lofgreen, A. M., Normand, P. S., Brennan, M. B., Rydberg, T. S., Boley, R. A., Pollack, M. H., & Niranjan, S. K. (2018). Evaluating patterns and predictors of symptom change during a three-week intensive outpatient treatment for veterans with PTSD. *BMC Psychiatry, 18*, 242. https://doi.org/10.1186/s12888-018-1816-6

Shahida Arabi, MA, is a published researcher and expert specializing in narcissism. She is a graduate of Harvard University and Columbia University, and holds graduate degrees in psychology and sociology. She is also author of several best-selling books, including *Becoming the Narcissist's Nightmare, The Highly Sensitive Person's Guide to Dealing with Toxic People,* and *Power.* Her books have been translated into more than eighteen languages all over the world. Her writing has been featured on *Salon, Bustle, Psychology Today, Huffington Post, VICE,* and *New York Daily News.* She lives in Manhattan, NY. Find out more about her at www.shahidaarabi .com.

Real change *is* possible

For more than fifty years, New Harbinger has published proven-effective self-help books and pioneering workbooks to help readers of all ages and backgrounds improve mental health and well-being, and achieve lasting personal growth. In addition, our spirituality books offer profound guidance for deepening awareness and cultivating healing, self-discovery, and fulfillment.

Founded by psychologist Matthew McKay and Patrick Fanning, New Harbinger is proud to be an independent, employee-owned company. Our books reflect our core values of integrity, innovation, commitment, sustainability, compassion, and trust. Written by leaders in the field and recommended by therapists worldwide, New Harbinger books are practical, accessible, and provide real tools for real change.

 **newharbinger**publications

MORE BOOKS from
NEW HARBINGER PUBLICATIONS

Did you know there are **free tools** you can download for this book?

Free tools are things like **worksheets, guided meditation exercises**, and **more** that will help you get the most out of your book.

You can download free tools for this book—whether you bought or borrowed it, in any format, from any source—from the New Harbinger website. All you need is a NewHarbinger.com account. Just use the URL provided in this book to view the free tools that are available for it. Then, click on the "download" button for the free tool you want, and follow the prompts that appear to log in to your NewHarbinger.com account and download the material.

You can also save the free tools for this book to your **Free Tools Library** so you can access them again anytime, just by logging in to your account! Just look for this button on the book's free tools page.

+ Save this to my free tools library

If you need help accessing or downloading free tools, visit **newharbinger.com/faq** or contact us at **customerservice@newharbinger.com.**